A Vegan Taste of India

Other titles in the series:

A Vegan Taste of India

Linda Majzlik

JON CARPENTER

Our books may be ordered from bookshops or (post free in the UK) from
Jon Carpenter Publishing, Alder House, Market Street, Charlbury,
England OX7 3PH

Please send for a catalogue

Credit card orders should be phoned or faxed to 01689 870437
or 01608 811969

First published in 2002 by
Jon Carpenter Publishing
Alder House, Market Street, Charlbury, England OX7 3PH
☎ 01608 811969

Reprinted 2006, 2008

ISBN 978-1-897766-75-0

Printed in England by The Cromwell Press, Trowbridge

CONTENTS

Rice

Breads

Main courses

Thali and side dishes

Desserts

Drinks

INTRODUCTION

Over the centuries India has been invaded and ruled by a number of tribes and nations, as a results of which it now has one of the most diverse populations in the world. With each new race that settled in India came new religions, cultures, customs and foods, and styles of cooking. Even today many dishes are prepared according to local traditions and religious beliefs and elaborate spreads are laid on at many of the festivals and celebrations that take place throughout the year. The preparation of food is central to family life and no unexpected guest is ever turned away without being fed. In fact it is seen as a great honour by many Indian families to share their mealtimes with guests.

As it is such a vast country, with a lot of regional variation in climate and agriculture, it comes as no surprise to find that the foods served in the far north differ from those found in the south or in other regions. However, the characteristic which brings dishes from all these areas together is the imaginative and subtle use of spices and herbs, which enhance rather than overpower the flavour of the other ingredients. Spices are also valued for their preservative, antiseptic and medicinal powers and cardamom, fennel or aniseed are often served at the end of a meal to aid digestion.

A typical meal in the north might consist of naan bread, baked in a tandoor, lightly spiced vegetables, and a rice dish containing fruit and nuts and served with dhal. Many northern dishes are cooked in a tandoor, which is a type of concave clay oven. Northern cuisine tends to be mildly spiced only and not nearly as hot as that in the south.

The city of Madras in southern India is famed for its blend of hot curry powder and many people believe that it is here that curries originated. Hot chillis, which were introduced by the Portuguese in the 16th century, grow in abundance in the area and they are added to most dishes. More rice is eaten in the south and dosas made from a rice and lentil paste are very popular here. Poppadums and lentil dishes such as sambar or dhal are favourite accompaniments or snacks all over the south.

Rajasthan in the central region of India is famed for its samosas and other spicy snacks, which are sold from roadside dhaba (stalls). Stuffed vegetable dishes, koftas and kebabs, reflecting an Islamic influence, are widely eaten in other central states. Many of the sweet desserts are believed to have originated in the eastern tea-growing state of Assam, perhaps a legacy from the days when the British ruled the country. These sweet dishes are however often eaten as snacks, rather than at the end of a meal.

Indian cuisine is very flexible and there are numerous ways of presenting a meal. Traditionally, a spicy appetiser or snack is served, followed by two or three spiced dishes, a dhal, and bread or a rice dish. These dishes are placed in the centre of the table for guests to help themselves to. Salads, chutney and raita are served as accompaniments. Alternatively, individual portions are placed in little bowls called katoris. Five or six bowls are filled with rice, spiced vegetable dishes, dhal, chutney and raita, and served on a large round tray, a thali. Each tray provides a complete meal. Indian foods are equally well suited to serving in the Western manner of starter, main course with accompaniments, followed by a dessert. When entertaining, Indian-style meals are an ideal choice as many spiced dishes actually benefit from being prepared in advance, to allow the flavours to develop. They can simply be reheated before serving.

Although three-quarters of India's vast population is believed to be vegetarian, they do rely heavily on dairy products. However, by using vegan substitutes for these it is possible to enjoy a truly authentic taste of India.

THE VEGAN INDIAN STORECUPBOARD

The following list contains some of the more commonly used ingredients in Indian cuisine, most of which are available from supermarkets or health food shops. If you are lucky enough to live near an Indian grocery store your visit will be rewarded with a wider range of products, especially beans and lentils, rice, fresh herbs and spices.

Almonds A favourite in Indian cuisine, almonds are used in a variety of dishes, both sweet and savoury. Almond-flavoured desserts are very popular, as are creamy savoury sauces made with ground almonds. Flaked almonds are added to rice dishes and used as garnish. As with most nuts, their flavour is enhanced if they are lightly toasted before use.

Beans and peas A highly nutritious staple food, both beans and peas are a good source of protein, fibre and minerals. Indian grocery stores stock a vast range of dried beans and peas and it is worth cooking them in bulk as they can be frozen successfully. Tinned beans and chickpeas are a useful standby.

Cashew nuts A member of the pulse family, cashew nuts are a good source of protein and minerals. Cashews are used in both savoury and sweet dishes and their flavour is greatly enhanced if they are lightly toasted.

Charoli nuts A small nut used in sweet dishes and in particular in the filling for sweet stuffed pastries. You may not be able to find charoli nuts other than in Indian grocery stores.

Coconut Used in various forms, coconut adds a creamy richness and flavour to sweet and savoury dishes.

Creamed This is pure fresh coconut flesh shaped into a vacuum-packed block. Once opened the block should be kept in the fridge and used within a couple of weeks.

Desiccated The dried flesh of the coconut is often used with other ingredients to made rich naan bread. It can also be used to make coconut milk.

Flaked Flakes of dried coconut are lightly toasted to enhance the flavour and then used to garnish sweet and savoury dishes.

Milk A rich thick liquid made from pressed coconut flesh, this is available tinned or in cartons. Coconut milk can also be made by dissolving 4oz/100g grated creamed coconut in 20 fl.oz/600ml hot water, or by blending 6oz/175g desiccated coconut with 20 fl.oz/600ml hot water and straining it through a fine sieve or muslin bag, pressing out as much liquid as possible. Any unused coconut milk can be frozen.

Cornflour A very fine starchy white flour which is milled from corn. It is sometimes known as cornstarch and is used to thicken sauces.

Flour Plain white and wholemeal, self-raising wholemeal and plain wholewheat flours are used to make a variety of dishes including sweet and savoury pastries, breads, batters and pancake mixtures.

Ginger, root An essential ingredient in Indian cookery, root ginger is used extensively to make various savoury dishes hotter and to add a spicy, fragrant flavour. To store root ginger, cut into portions, wrap individually in foil and freeze.

Ginger, stem Stem ginger preserved in sugar syrup is available in jars. This sweetened version makes a popular addition to fresh fruit salads and is used in many chutney recipes.

Gram flour Also called bessan, this fine yellowy nutritious flour is made from chickpeas. It is used as a thickener and for batters and pancakes.

Ground rice White rice which has been milled to a grainy powder, ground rice is the main ingredient in kheer, a favourite sweet Indian dish. It is also used occasionally in savoury dishes.

Herbs Although herbs are not used nearly as much as spices in Indian cuisine, specific herbs are considered essential for flavouring certain dishes.

Basil The type used in Indian cooking is known as holy basil and may only be available in Indian grocery stores. Ordinary basil can serve as a substitute and this herb has a natural affinity with tomatoes.

Bay leaves These aromatic dark green leaves of an evergreen tree are best used dried, to impart their distinct, strong and slightly bitter flavour to various rice dishes.

Coriander Fresh coriander leaves are widely used as an ingredient and as garnish. The herb's unique taste and aroma gives many dishes their distinctive Indian flavour.

Curry leaves These aromatic curry-flavoured leaves may be used either fresh or dried. Fresh leaves have more flavour and they can be stored in the freezer.

Mint The Moghuls were responsible for introducing mint to the Indian subcontinent. The leaves are always used fresh and mint is a vital ingredient in some raita recipes. Whole leaves are often used to garnish fruit salads and drinks.

Mixed herbs A mixture of several sweet herbs and an essential flavouring for onion and nut pakodas.

Parsley A universally popular herb, parsley is sometimes used as a garnish rather than as an ingredient.

Lemon grass Available in many forms, fresh, dried, ground, bottled, chopped or as a purée. Lemon grass adds a fragrant yet subtle lemony flavour and aroma to savoury dishes.

Lentils A staple food which is grown and used throughout Asia. Lentils come in various colours and each type has its own particular characteristics and taste. All lentils are highly nutritious and they are used extensively to make soothing soups and spicy dhals.

Millet A highly nutritious mild-flavoured grain, which is a staple ingredient in some parts of India. It can be used instead of rice and is a perfect foil for rich spicy foods.

Peanuts Also known as groundnuts, this popular but inexpensive nut is a very good source of protein, minerals and vitamins. Spiced peanuts are a favourite snack food in many regions. They are also used as an ingredient and for garnishing many savoury dishes.

Peanut butter Both smooth and crunchy unsweetened versions are used to add richness to hotpots, sauces and curries.

Pistachio nuts These light green flavourful nuts are sold in their split shells or ready shelled, either salted or unsalted. Salted pistachios are a popular snack food, while the unsalted nuts are used in savoury and sweet dishes. They also make as a colourful garnish.

Rice Many different types of rice are grown throughout Asia and in certain areas a meal is considered incomplete without a rice dish of some sort. Rice is a valuable staple food and a good source of vitamins and minerals. The following varieties are the most popular:

Basmati A slender-grained, highly aromatic rice which is grown in Northern India and Pakistan. Basmati is available as white or brown grains and both give an authentic flavour and aroma to Indian rice dishes.

Long grain Available as white or brown grains. Brown rice has a slightly nutty, chewier texture and takes longer to cook than white. It also contains more fibre, vitamins and minerals than the white variety, which has had the bran, germ and husk removed in the milling process.

Patna A slightly fatter and starchier long grain rice which is grown in the Bengal region.

Soya milk Unsweetened soya milk has been used in both sweet and savoury recipes.

Spices Spices are of paramount importance in Indian cuisine and a combination of many or as few as a couple are used to enhance the flavours of the foods being cooked. As ground spices quickly go stale and lose their flavour, they are best bought in small quantities and stored in a cool dark cupboard. Indian cooks always grind their own spices freshly in a mortar with a pestle for each meal. Spices are invariably fried briefly or dry roasted to bring out their full flavours before the main ingredients are added.

Cardamom This pine-fragranced spice is available in three forms: pods, seeds or ground. The pods vary in colour, but it is generally agreed that the green variety has more flavour and aroma. Cardamom is a popular spice not only in savoury but especially in sweet dishes. The seeds are also often chewed after a meal to aid digestion and freshen the breath.

Chilli powder Chillis, when dried and ground, are very hot and the powder adds instant heat to savoury dishes.

Cinnamon Used in sticks or ground, cinnamon has a warm, comforting, sweet flavour which makes it a very versatile spice and ideal for adding to both sweet and savoury dishes.

Cloves These dried buds of an evergreen tree are valued for their anaesthetic and antiseptic properties. Whole cloves are often added to savoury rice dishes and they are also used to flavour fruit salads and masala tea.

Coriander Used ground and as whole seeds, coriander has a mild citrus flavour and is a main ingredient in curry powder blends. Ground coriander quickly loses its flavour, so it is best to grind the whole seeds with a pestle in a mortar or, more easily, in a peppermill.

Cumin Sometimes referred to as the most Indian of spices, cumin is used both ground and as seeds. The slightly bitter tasting seeds can be dry roasted before use. Cumin is valued as a digestive, so it is often added to dishes containing beans.

Curry powder/paste In India there is no such thing as a ready-made curry powder or paste, as Indian cooks always prepare their own special blends from the various whole spices available. The commercially-prepared blends of powders and pastes we are able to buy vary from very mild to extremely hot. As a basic guide, korma is generally the mildest, while Madras mixes are medium hot and vindaloos are the hottest.

Fenugreek Available as whole seeds or ground, fenugreek is valued for its ability to soothe the intestines. Ground fenugreek has a bitter-sweet flavour and is always used sparingly. It is also thought to enhance the flavours of the other spices. The seeds are frequently used in rice dishes and are usually fried first to temper the flavour.

Garam masala A blend of several ground spices usually consisting of black pepper, cinnamon, cloves, coriander and cumin. Ready-made blends are available, but many Indian cooks grind their own mixes to traditional family recipes. Garam masala is used in various savoury recipes as well as for garnishing dishes.

Ginger The dried ground root is an ingredient in some curry powder mixes. It has a strong, spicy but sweet flavour which is equally suited to savoury and to sweet dishes.

Mace The hard, lacy outer covering of the nutmeg kernel, mace and nutmeg are the only two spices to come from one tree. Mace has a similar but milder flavour to nutmeg and can be used as a substitute for it. Mace and nutmeg go especially well with green vegetables.

Mango powder Also known as amchoor, this spice is ground from dried, unripe, sour mangoes. Mango powder adds a slightly sweet sharpness to savoury dishes. It may only be available from Indian grocery stores.

Mustard seed These come in three colours, yellow (sometimes called white), brown and black. Dry roasting or frying in a little oil until they pop brings out the full flavour of the seeds. They are especially good for flavouring dhals and rice dishes.

Nutmeg The sweet, spicy seed of an evergreen tropical tree. Nutmeg is available as whole seeds for grating or ready-ground. Special nutmeg graters can be bought to grate the seeds.

Onion seed These crunchy, black seeds are also called kalonji and have a pleasant mild oniony flavour. They are used in particular for sprinkling on breads and pastry dishes.

Panchphoran A traditional Bengali spice mixture containing black mustard, cumin, fennel, fenugreek and onion seeds in equal proportion.

Paprika The dried ground pod of a sweet red pepper adds colour and a mild sweet flavour to soups, dhals and vegetable dishes. It goes particularly well with tomatoes.

Pepper A universally popular seasoning for savoury dishes. Freshly ground black peppercorns are preferred.

Saffron The most expensive of all the spices available, saffron consists of the dried stigmas of a variety of crocus. Luckily, only a small amount is required to impart colour and a pungent, slightly bitter, yet aromatic taste, especially to rice dishes.

Turmeric This native bright-yellow spice is the powdered rhizome of a plant belonging to the ginger family. It is valued for its anti-bacterial properties and adds colour and an earthy flavour to vegetable and rice dishes.

Tamarind The fruit of a large tropical tree, tamarind is used to add sourness to savoury dishes. It is usually sold in a sticky block consisting of crushed pods, which needs to be soaked in hot water to produce a purée. Jars of ready-made purée are also available.

Textured vegetable protein A nutritious and versatile soya product which readily absorbs the flavours of the other ingredients. Natural, unflavoured chunks and mince are used in various savoury recipes.

Tinned tomatoes Fresh tomatoes are used in preference to tinned, but there are a few recipes which actually benefit from the extra taste that the tinned variety has.

Tomato purée Used to strengthen the flavour of and add colour to tomato-based dishes. Tomato purée should be used sparingly - too much can give a slightly acidic taste.

Vegetable oils In some regions mustard oil is favoured, although any good quality vegetable oil is suitable for frying and for making salad dressings.

Vegetable stock Used in a variety of savoury recipes, vegetable stock is easy to make and adds a more authentic flavour than stock cubes. It can be made in bulk and frozen in measured quantities. Peel and chop a selection of vegetables such as carrots, celery, green beans, onions, potatoes and sweet potatoes. Put them in a large pan and add a couple of chopped garlic cloves and a chopped green chilli (optional), a few sprigs of fresh parsley and a bay leaf. Cover with water and bring to the boil. Cover the pan and simmer for 30 minutes. Strain the liquid through a fine sieve.

Vinegar Light malt vinegar is used in chutney recipes and for salad dressings, as it is mildly flavoured and does not mask the flavours of the main ingredients.

Yeast Most Indian breads are unleavened but easy-blend yeast is used in the recipe for naan bread. It does not need to be reconstituted in liquid.

Yoghurt Yoghurt is such a vital ingredient that it is made on a daily basis by many Indian cooks. Plain soya yoghurt is an excellent substitute, which can be added to a variety of recipes from savoury snacks and spicy sauces to refreshing raitas, drinks and sweet desserts.

SNACKS AND STARTERS

Indian snacks, known as chaat, are legendary and streets in the towns and cities abound with stalls selling a great variety of spicy bits and pieces. They are eaten at any time of day and are usually accompanied by chutney or raita. The recipes included here can also be used as starters or as part of a light lunch or main meal. All these snacks make ideal party food and they can be made in advance and reheated when required.

Aubergine samosas *(makes 16)*

pastry

8oz/225g plain wholemeal flour

2oz/50g vegan margarine

1 teaspoon turmeric

approx. 4 fl.oz/125ml soya milk

vegetable oil

filling

8oz/225g aubergine, finely chopped

2oz/50g tomato, skinned and finely chopped

2oz/50g cooked black-eye beans

1 onion, peeled and finely chopped

1 garlic clove, crushed

½ inch/1cm piece of root ginger, peeled and finely chopped

2 tablespoons vegetable oil

1 teaspoon ground coriander

¼ teaspoon ground cinnamon

¼ teaspoon chilli powder

black pepper

Mix the turmeric with the flour and rub in the margarine. Gradually add the soya milk until a soft dough forms. Knead well, then chill for 1 hour.

Heat the oil for the filling and gently fry the aubergine, onion, garlic and ginger for 10 minutes, stirring frequently. Add the spices, tomato and black-eye beans and combine well. Raise the heat and cook for a further 5 minutes, until the aubergine is tender and the mixture is thick. Stir frequently to prevent sticking.

Divide the pastry into 8 equal portions. Roll each one into a 6 inch/15cm diameter circle and cut each circle in half. Divide the filling equally between the pastry halves, placing it neatly on one side only. Dampen the pastry edges with water, fold the pastry over and press the edges together to enclose the filling. Fry the samosas in hot vegetable oil until golden. Drain on kitchen paper.

Parsnip and almond koftas   *(makes 16)*

12oz/350g parsnip, peeled

4oz/100g ground almonds

1oz/25g natural minced textured vegetable protein

5 fl.oz/150ml hot vegetable stock

1 onion, peeled and finely chopped

1 dessertspoon vegetable oil

1 teaspoon ground coriander

½ teaspoon ground cumin

¼ teaspoon turmeric

black pepper

flour

extra vegetable oil

Soak the vegetable protein in the stock for 1 hour. Drain and squeeze out any excess liquid with the back of a spoon. Cut the parsnip into even-sized chunks and boil for 10 minutes. Drain, allow to cool, then grate. Heat the dessertspoonful of oil in a large pan and gently fry the onion until softened. Add the spices and fry for 1 minute more. Remove from the heat and add the vegetable protein, parsnip and almonds. Mix thoroughly, take rounded dessertspoonfuls and roll into balls in the palm of the hand. Lightly roll each ball in flour to cover and put them on a plate. Cover and chill for 2 hours. Deep fry in hot vegetable oil for about 5 minutes until golden brown and drain on kitchen paper.

Spicy chickpeas   *(serves 4)*

14oz/400g tin cooked chickpeas, drained and rinsed

6oz/175g tomato, skinned and chopped

4oz/100g red pepper, chopped

1oz/25g mushrooms, wiped and chopped

1 onion, peeled and finely chopped

1 garlic clove, crushed

1 tablespoon vegetable oil

1 teaspoon cumin seed

½ teaspoon ground fenugreek

¼ teaspoon chilli powder

½ inch/1cm stick of cinnamon, crumbled

4 cardamoms, husked and the seeds separated

black pepper

finely chopped fresh coriander leaves

Heat the oil and fry the onion, garlic and red pepper for about 10 minutes until soft. Add the mushrooms and spices and fry for another minute, then add the tomato and cook gently until pulpy. Stir in the chickpeas and continue cooking for a few minutes more, stirring all the time. Transfer to little serving bowls and garnish with chopped fresh coriander.

Savoury nimki   *(serves 4/6)*

6oz/175g plain flour

½ oz/15g vegan margarine

½ teaspoon salt

1 teaspoon black onion seed

1 teaspoon cumin seed

½ teaspoon turmeric

black pepper

water

vegetable oil

Sift the flour, salt and turmeric into a mixing bowl. Rub in the margarine and stir in the onion and cumin seed. Season with black pepper and add enough water to make a soft dough. Knead well, then roll out thinly on a floured board. Cut the dough into small diamond shapes and prick the tops with a fork. Fry the shapes in hot vegetable oil until golden. Drain on kitchen paper and serve.

Savoury pancakes *(serves 4)*

4oz/100g plain wholemeal flour

2oz/50g gram flour

8 fl.oz/225ml soya milk

2 rounded tablespoons plain soya yoghurt

½ oz/15g creamed coconut, grated

1 onion, peeled and finely chopped

2 garlic cloves, crushed

1 small red chilli, finely chopped

2oz/50g mushrooms, wiped and finely chopped

2oz/50g sweetcorn kernels

1 tablespoon finely chopped fresh coriander leaves

1 rounded teaspoon garam masala

½ teaspoon turmeric

vegetable oil

Sift the two flours with the garam masala and turmeric into a large bowl. Add the soya milk, yoghurt and coconut and mix until smooth, then the remaining ingredients apart from the vegetable oil and combine thoroughly. Heat a small amount of vegetable oil in a non-stick frying pan and fry rounded tablespoonfuls of the mixture for a few minutes on each side until browned.

Potato and pea patties   *(makes 16)*

2lb/900g potatoes, peeled and cut into even-sized chunks

4oz/100g frozen peas, cooked and drained

1 onion, peeled and chopped

1 garlic clove, chopped

1 teaspoon cumin seed

2 rounded tablespoons finely chopped fresh coriander

black pepper

vegetable oil

coating

3oz/75g breadcrumbs

½ teaspoon turmeric

black pepper

1½oz/40g gram flour

4 tablespoons water

Boil the potatoes for 10 minutes, drain and allow to cool. Grate them into a mixing bowl and add the peas, cumin seeds and coriander. Mince the onion with the garlic and add to the bowl. Season with black pepper and mix thoroughly. Take rounded tablespoonfuls of the mixture and shape into flat rounds.

Mix the gram flour with the water until smooth, then brush the potato rounds all over with this paste. Mix the turmeric with the breadcrumbs and season with black pepper. Dip each coated potato round in the breadcrumbs until it is completely covered. Shake off excess crumbs and shallow fry the patties in hot vegetable oil for a few minutes on each side until golden brown. Drain on kitchen paper.

Vegetable pakoras   *(serves 4)*

> approx. 1lb/450g mixed prepared vegetables (peppers, aubergine, courgette, onion, cauliflower, broccoli, etc.), cut into even-sized chunks
>
> vegetable oil
>
> ***batter***
>
> 5oz/150g gram flour
>
> 4 fl.oz/125ml water
>
> 2 tablespoons plain soya yoghurt
>
> 1 dessertspoon lemon juice
>
> 1 rounded dessertspoon mild curry paste

Whisk the batter ingredients together until smooth. Dip the vegetable chunks in the batter, allowing any excess to drain off. Deep fry in hot vegetable oil until golden and drain on kitchen paper.

Spiced peanuts and raisins   *(serves 4/6)*

> 8oz/225g shelled blanched peanuts
>
> 2oz/50g raisins
>
> 1 tablespoon vegetable oil
>
> ½ teaspoon ground coriander
>
> ½ teaspoon ground cumin
>
> ¼ teaspoon turmeric
>
> ¼ teaspoon garam masala

Mix the spices with the oil and add the peanuts. Stir well until the nuts are evenly coated. Put them in a baking tin and bake in a preheated oven at 170°C/325°F/Gas mark 3 for 15-20 minutes until golden, stirring occasionally to ensure even browning. Add the raisins, then allow to cool before serving.

Spiced potato and spinach wheels   *(makes 12)*

2lb/900g potatoes, peeled

4oz/100g wholemeal self-raising flour

1oz/25g vegan margarine

½ teaspoon turmeric

black pepper

filling

8oz/225g fresh spinach, washed and finely shredded

1 onion, peeled and finely chopped

2 garlic cloves, crushed

1 tablespoon vegetable oil

1 rounded tablespoon plain soya yoghurt

1 teaspoon garam masala

1 teaspoon black mustard seed

black pepper

extra vegetable oil

Cut the potatoes into even-sized chunks and boil until done, then drain and dry off over a low heat. Mash the potatoes with the margarine and add the sifted flour and turmeric. Season with black pepper and mix thoroughly. Chill for 1 hour.

Heat the tablespoonful of oil in a large pan and gently fry the onion and garlic until soft. Add the mustard seed and garam masala and fry for 1 minute more. Squeeze any excess water from the spinach and add to the pan. Cook for 10-15 minutes until tender, stirring occasionally to prevent sticking. Remove from the heat and add the yoghurt. Season with black pepper and mix well. Allow to cool.

Turn the potato mixture out onto a floured piece of cling film and shape or roll into a 12 x 9 inch/30 x 23cm oblong. Spread the spinach mixture evenly over the base, leaving a 1 inch/2.5cm gap along one of the long edges for sealing. Starting from the other long edge roll up like a Swiss roll (using the cling film to pull the roll up makes this easier) and squeeze the edges together to join. Cut the roll into 12 1 inch/2.5cm portions with a sharp knife and shallow fry the wheels for a few minutes on each side until browned. Drain on kitchen paper before serving.

Mung bean and pistachio fritters   *(serves 4)*

4oz/100g mung beans

2oz/50g shelled pistachio nuts, ground

1 small onion, grated

2oz/50g gram flour

½ teaspoon garam masala

black pepper

vegetable oil

Soak the mung beans overnight in water. Drain and put them in a fresh pan of water. Bring to the boil, cover and simmer until soft. Drain well, then mash the beans with the back of a spoon or a potato masher until smooth. Add the ground nuts, onion, gram flour and garam masala, season with black pepper and mix thoroughly. Take heaped teaspoonfuls of the mixture and shape into small flattish balls. Shallow fry in hot oil until golden. Drain on kitchen paper.

Dosas   *(makes 8)*

8oz/225g long grain white rice

2oz/50g red lentils

1 teaspoon bicarbonate of soda

1 teaspoon ground cumin

½ teaspoon salt

¼ teaspoon chilli powder

black pepper

vegetable oil

Wash the rice and lentils thoroughly, then cover with water and leave to soak for an hour. Drain and pour into a blender. Add water until the rice and lentils are just covered, then blend until smooth. Transfer to a jug and add the bicarbonate of soda, cumin, salt and chilli powder. Whisk well, cover and leave overnight or for at least 8 hours.

Heat 1 teaspoonful of oil in a heavy-based 6 inch/15cm frying pan until hot. Whisk the mixture, then put 3 tablespoonfuls into the pan and swirl around until the base is covered. Fry for a few minutes until golden brown underneath, carefully turn over and fry the other side. Repeat with the remaining mixture. Serve plain or with a savoury filling.

Mushroom and almond kebabs   *(serves 6)*

4oz/100g mushrooms, wiped and finely chopped

4oz/100g ground almonds

2oz/50g natural minced textured vegetable protein

2oz/50g gram flour

2oz/50g plain wholemeal flour

1 onion, peeled and chopped

1 inch/2.5cm piece of root ginger, peeled and chopped

2 garlic cloves

8 fl.oz/225ml hot vegetable stock

1 tablespoon vegetable oil

½ teaspoon mango powder

½ teaspoon cumin seed

¼ teaspoon turmeric

¼ teaspoon ground fenugreek

¼ teaspoon chilli powder

black pepper

extra vegetable oil

Mince the onion with the ginger and garlic, then fry in the tablespoonful of oil until soft. Add the spices and stir around for 1 minute. Remove from the heat and stir in the vegetable protein and stock. Cover and leave to soak for an hour. Add the remaining ingredients and mix well until everything binds together. Lightly grease 12 small square skewers. Divide the mixture into 12 equal portions and squeeze each portion neatly around one of the skewers. Brush the kebabs with oil and transfer to a baking tray. Place under a hot grill for about 15 minutes, turning occasionally, until golden brown.

Marrow and nut cutlets   (serves 6)

1 lb/450g marrow flesh, washed, dried and grated

1 onion, peeled and finely chopped

2 garlic cloves, crushed

½ inch/1cm piece of root ginger, peeled and finely chopped

4oz/100g mixed nuts, grated

2oz/50g gram flour

2oz/50g plain wholemeal flour

1 rounded teaspoon ground coriander

1 rounded teaspoon cumin seed

½ teaspoon paprika

½ teaspoon turmeric

¼ teaspoon ground fenugreek

pinch of ground chilli powder

black pepper

vegetable oil

extra wholemeal flour

Put the marrow, onion, garlic, ginger and grated nuts in a bowl and stir. Add the sifted flours and spices and mix thoroughly until it all binds together. Take rounded dessertspoonfuls of the mixture and roll into balls. Flatten each ball slightly and roll in wholemeal flour until coated all over. Put on a plate, cover and chill for a couple of hours. Shallow fry the cutlets in hot vegetable oil for a few minutes on each side until golden and drain on kitchen paper.

Potato bhajias   *(serves 4)*

1¼ lb/550g potatoes, scraped

1 onion, peeled and grated

1 inch/2.5cm piece of root ginger, peeled and finely chopped

1 green chilli, finely chopped (optional)

1 rounded tablespoon finely chopped fresh coriander

1 rounded teaspoon curry powder

black pepper

vegetable oil

batter

4oz/100g gram flour

½ teaspoon turmeric

4 fl.oz/125ml water

Cook the potatoes, drain and chop finely. Put them in a mixing bowl and add the onion, ginger, chilli, coriander and curry powder. Season with black pepper and mix very well. Take rounded dessertspoonfuls of the mixture and shape into small balls.

Sift the turmeric with the gram flour, add the water and mix until smooth. Dip the potato balls in the batter to coat them, then deep fry in hot vegetable oil for a few minutes until browned. Drain on kitchen paper and serve.

Lentil and cashew koftas   *(serves 6)*

8oz/225g red lentils

4oz/100g cashew nuts, ground

4oz/100g carrot, scraped and grated

2oz/50g plain wholemeal flour

2oz/50g gram flour

1 onion, peeled and chopped

1 garlic clove

1 teaspoon ground cumin

1 teaspoon tamarind purée

½ teaspoon ground cinnamon

½ teaspoon paprika

pinch of ground chilli powder

black pepper

vegetable oil

Soak the lentils for 2 hours. Drain and put in a fresh pan of water. Bring to the boil, cover and simmer for about 15 minutes until tender, then pour into a fine sieve and leave for about 30 minutes until all the liquid has drained off. Mince the onion with the garlic, transfer to a mixing bowl and add the drained lentils and all remaining ingredients, except the vegetable oil. Mix thoroughly, then take rounded dessertspoonfuls of the mixture and shape into balls in the palm of the hand. Fry them in hot vegetable oil until golden brown and drain on kitchen paper.

Onion and nut pakodas *(serves 4)*

12oz/350g onion, peeled and grated

4oz/100g ground rice

2oz/50g gram flour

2oz/50g plain wholemeal flour

2oz/50g mixed nuts, ground

1 rounded teaspoon mixed herbs

½ teaspoon turmeric

½ teaspoon garam masala

black pepper

water

vegetable oil

Mix the ground rice with the gram and wholemeal flours, ground nuts, herbs, turmeric and garam masala in a large bowl. Stir in the onion and season with black pepper, then add enough water to make a thick batter. Fry rounded dessertspoonfuls of the mixture in hot vegetable oil until golden.

DHALS AND SOUPS

A trip to an Indian grocery store will reveal that there are literally dozens of different beans and lentils available, and these form a very important part of the Indian diet. No thali is ever complete without a little bowl of dhal, a nourishing thick soup-like accompaniment. In the south of India a lentil and vegetable soup called sambar is a regional favourite, traditionally served with dosas or plain boiled rice. Soups are eaten at any time of the day, either as a snack, served with bread or rice, or as an appetiser before a main course. Cooked dhals are sometimes thinned with water and used as a thin soup.

Tomato and red lentil dhal   *(serves 4)*

4oz/100g tomatoes, skinned and chopped

4oz/100g red lentils

1 onion, peeled and finely chopped

2 garlic cloves, crushed

1 tablespoon vegetable oil

1 teaspoon black mustard seed

1 teaspoon ground cumin

½ teaspoon paprika

pinch of chilli powder

black pepper

1 dessertspoon tomato purée

15 fl.oz/450ml water

Soak the lentils in water for 30 minutes. Heat the oil in a pan and gently fry the onion and garlic until softened. Add the mustard seed, cumin, paprika and chilli powder and fry for 30 seconds, then add the tomatoes and cook until pulpy. Dissolve the tomato purée in the water and add to the pan together with the drained lentils. Season with black pepper and stir well. Bring to the boil, cover and simmer for about 30 minutes, stirring occasionally, until the lentils are soft and the mixture thickens.

Mung bean dhal   *(serves 4)*

4oz/100g mung beans

1 onion, peeled and finely chopped

1 garlic clove, crushed

1 small green chilli, finely chopped

1 tablespoon vegetable oil

1 teaspoon ground cumin

1 teaspoon ground coriander

1 teaspoon black mustard seed

¼ teaspoon ground fenugreek

4 cardamoms, husked and the seeds separated

black pepper

25 fl.oz/750ml vegetable stock or water

finely chopped fresh parsley

Soak the mung beans in water for 2 hours. Heat the oil and fry the onion, garlic and chilli until soft. Add the cumin, coriander, mustard seed, fenugreek and cardamoms and stir around for 30 seconds. Drain the mung beans and add them to the pan together with the stock or water. Season with black pepper and bring to the boil. Cover and simmer for about 50 minutes, stirring occasionally, until the beans are tender. Remove from the heat and mash with a potato masher. Return to the stove and heat gently, whilst stirring, for a minute or two. Garnish with chopped parsley when serving.

Spinach and green lentil dhal   (serves 4)

8oz/225g fresh spinach, finely chopped

4oz/100g green lentils

1 onion, peeled and finely chopped

1 garlic clove, crushed

½ oz/15g vegan margarine

1 rounded tablespoon chopped fresh coriander leaves

1 rounded teaspoon ground cumin

1 rounded teaspoon ground coriander

¼ teaspoon grated nutmeg

4 cardamoms, husked and the seeds separated

black pepper

Soak the lentils for 2 hours, then drain and rinse and put in a fresh pan of water. Bring to the boil, cover and simmer briskly for 15 minutes. Drain and keep 8 fl.oz/225ml of the cooking water.

Melt the margarine in a large saucepan and soften the onion and garlic. Add the cumin, coriander, nutmeg and cardamoms and stir around for 30 seconds. Add the spinach and cook gently for 3 minutes while stirring. Now add the lentils, cooking water and coriander. Season with black pepper and stir well. Bring to the boil, cover and simmer for about 35 minutes, stirring occasionally, until the lentils are tender and the mixture thickens.

Mushroom and brown lentil dhal   *(serves 4)*

8oz/225g mushrooms, wiped and chopped

4oz/100g brown lentils

1 onion, peeled and finely chopped

1 garlic clove, crushed

1 tablespoon vegetable oil

1 tablespoon finely chopped fresh coriander leaves

1 teaspoon ground cumin

1 teaspoon ground coriander

½ teaspoon garam masala

black pepper

Soak the lentils for 2 hours, rinse and bring to the boil in fresh water. Cover and boil rapidly for 15 minutes. Drain the lentils over a bowl and keep the cooking liquid.

Heat the oil in a pan and gently fry the onion and garlic until soft. Add the mushrooms and fry for 2 minutes more, then the cumin, coriander, garam masala and coriander leaves and stir around for 30 seconds. Add the drained lentils together with 12 fl.oz/350ml of the cooking water. Season with black pepper and stir well. Bring to the boil, cover and simmer for about 30 minutes, stirring occasionally, until the liquid has been absorbed and the lentils are soft.

Chickpea dhal   *(serves 4)*

8oz/225g cooked chickpeas, grated

8oz/225g tin crushed tomatoes

1 onion, peeled and finely chopped

2 garlic cloves, crushed

½ inch/1cm piece of root ginger, peeled and finely chopped

1 small red chilli, finely chopped

2 fl.oz/50ml water

1 tablespoon vegetable oil

few curry leaves

½ teaspoon cumin seed

½ teaspoon yellow mustard seed

¼ teaspoon ground fenugreek

¼ teaspoon paprika

black pepper

2 spring onions, trimmed and sliced

Heat the oil and gently soften the onion, garlic, ginger and chilli. Add the cumin and mustard seed, fenugreek and paprika and fry for 30 seconds more. Add the tomatoes, chickpeas, water and curry leaves and season with black pepper. Stir well and bring to the boil, then simmer for 5 minutes while stirring occasionally. Transfer to a serving dish and garnish with sliced spring onions.

Sambar *(serves 4)*

8oz/225g potato, peeled and diced

8oz/225g carrot, scraped and diced

4oz/100g brown lentils

4oz/100g green beans, topped, tailed and chopped

2oz/50g mushrooms, wiped and chopped

1 onion, peeled and finely chopped

1 red chilli, finely chopped

1 inch/2.5cm piece of root ginger, peeled and finely chopped

1oz/25g creamed coconut, grated

30 fl.oz/900ml vegetable stock

1 tablespoon vegetable oil

1 teaspoon cumin seed

1 teaspoon black mustard seed

½ teaspoon turmeric

¼ teaspoon ground coriander

¼ teaspoon ground fenugreek

½ inch/1cm stick of cinnamon

black pepper

chopped fresh coriander leaves

Soak the brown lentils in water for 2 hours, wash, drain and set aside. Heat the oil in a large pan and gently fry the onion, chilli and ginger until softened. Add the cumin and mustard seed, turmeric, ground coriander, fenugreek and cinnamon and stir around for 30 seconds. Add the lentils and stock and combine well. Bring to the boil, then cover and simmer gently for about 45 minutes, stirring occasionally, until the lentils are soft. Steam the potato, carrot and green beans until just tender and add to the pan with the mushrooms and creamed coconut. Season with black pepper and stir until the coconut dissolves. Simmer for 5 minutes whilst stirring, garnish with chopped fresh coriander and serve.

Tomato soup   *(serves 4)*

8oz/225g ripe tomatoes, skinned and chopped

1 onion, peeled and finely chopped

4 garlic cloves, crushed

½ oz/15g vegan margarine

20 fl.oz/600ml water

1 dessertspoon tamarind purée

1 dessertspoon sugar

1 teaspoon curry leaves

1 teaspoon ground cumin

½ teaspoon paprika

black pepper

chopped fresh coriander leaves

Fry the onion and garlic in the margarine until soft. Add the cumin and paprika and stir around for 30 seconds, then add the tomatoes and cook until pulpy. Stir in the remaining ingredients apart from the chopped coriander, and bring to the boil. Cover and simmer for 10 minutes. Allow to cool slightly, then liquidise until smooth. When serving garnish with chopped fresh coriander.

Vegetable and coconut soup   *(serves 4)*

4oz/100g potatoes, peeled and diced

4oz/100g courgette, chopped

3oz/75g cauliflower, cut into small florets

3oz/75g carrot, scraped and thinly sliced

2oz/50g cooked black-eye beans

1oz/25g shelled peas

1oz/25g sweetcorn kernels

½ oz/15g sultanas

2 celery sticks, trimmed and sliced

2 garlic cloves, crushed

1 onion, peeled and sliced

1oz/25g creamed coconut, grated

22 fl.oz/650ml vegetable stock

2 fl.oz/50ml soya milk

1 tablespoon gram flour

1 tablespoon vegetable oil

1 rounded teaspoon curry powder

1 teaspoon yellow mustard seed

½ teaspoon turmeric

2 cardamoms, husked and the seeds separated

black pepper

toasted flaked coconut

Heat the oil in a large pan and gently fry the celery, garlic and onion until soft. Add the curry powder, mustard seed, turmeric and cardamom and stir around for 30 seconds. Dissolve the creamed coconut in the vegetable stock and add to the pan together with the vegetables and sultanas. Season with black pepper and stir well. Bring to the boil, cover and simmer for about 25 minutes until the vegetables are just tender. Dissolve the gram flour in the soya milk and add to the pan. Raise the heat and stir for a minute or two until the soup thickens. Garnish with toasted flaked coconut.

Brown rice and lentil soup   *(serves 4)*

4oz/100g long grain brown rice

4oz/100g red lentils

4oz/100g mushrooms, wiped and finely chopped

1 onion, peeled and finely chopped

3 garlic cloves, crushed

1 tablespoon vegetable oil

32 fl.oz/950ml vegetable stock

1 teaspoon ground coriander

¼ teaspoon ground cinnamon

¼ teaspoon ground cardamom

black pepper

chopped fresh parsley

Heat the oil and gently soften the onion and garlic. Add the mushrooms, coriander, cinnamon and cardamom and fry for 1 minute more. Stir in the remaining ingredients apart from the parsley, and bring to the boil. Cover and simmer for about 25 minutes, stirring occasionally, until the rice and lentils are done. Garnish the soup with chopped fresh parsley when serving.

RICE

Rice has been grown in India for about 6,000 years and it is eaten by most Indians daily, either plain or with the addition of vegetables, fruits and nuts. Basmati is considered to be the best and most aromatic rice and it gives an authentic flavour to many Indian rice dishes. Other suitable types include white and brown long grain rice and patna, which is slightly fatter and starchier. To remove the starch and prevent the grains from sticking together it is best to rinse the rice in several changes of water before cooking. Any leftover rice dishes can be refrigerated and eaten cold as salad.

Vegetable pilau   *(serves 4)*

12oz/350 prepared mixed vegetables, chopped

8oz/225g basmati rice

1oz/25g sultanas

1 onion, peeled and finely chopped

2 garlic cloves, crushed

1 inch/2.5cm piece of root ginger, peeled and finely chopped

1 inch/2.5cm stick of cinnamon

1 bay leaf

4 cloves

6 cardamoms, husked and the seeds separated

½ teaspoon turmeric

½ teaspoon fenugreek seed

½ teaspoon yellow mustard seed

1 teaspoon cumin seed

1 tablespoon vegan margarine

20 fl.oz/600ml water

black pepper

chopped fresh coriander leaves

tomato wedges

Melt the margarine in a large pan and fry the onion, garlic and ginger until soft. Add the spices and rice and stir around for 2 minutes. Now add the remaining ingredients, except the coriander and tomato, and stir well. Bring to the boil, cover and simmer gently until the liquid has been absorbed and the vegetables and rice are cooked. Transfer to a warmed serving dish and garnish with the chopped coriander leaves and the tomato wedges.

Spiced sweetcorn rice *(serves 4)*

8oz/225g basmati rice

8oz/225g sweetcorn kernels

1 tablespoon vegetable oil

1 rounded teaspoon cumin seed

1 rounded teaspoon yellow mustard seed

½ inch/1cm stick of cinnamon, crushed

¼ teaspoon turmeric

2 cloves

black pepper

18 fl.oz/550ml water

Dry roast the cumin and yellow mustard seed in a heavy-based pan. Add the oil and the rice and fry gently for 1 minute. Add the remaining ingredients and stir well. Bring to the boil, cover and simmer until the liquid has been absorbed and the rice is tender.

Tomato and black-eye bean rice *(serves 4)*

8oz/225g long grain rice

4oz/100g cooked black-eye beans

14oz/400g tin chopped tomatoes

1 onion, peeled and finely chopped

1 celery stick, trimmed and finely sliced

2 garlic cloves, crushed

12 fl.oz/350ml water

1 tablespoon vegetable oil

1 dessertspoon tamarind purée

1 teaspoon cumin seed

½ teaspoon paprika

black pepper

chopped fresh basil leaves

1 tomato, sliced

Soften the onion, celery and garlic in the oil in a large pan. Add the rice, cumin seed and paprika and stir around for 1 minute. Remove from the heat and stir in the remaining ingredients apart from the basil and the tomato. Cover and leave for 15 minutes, then return to the heat and bring to the boil. Cover and simmer very gently, until the liquid has been absorbed and the rice is cooked. Spoon into a warmed serving dish and garnish with chopped basil and tomato slices.

Spinach and courgette rice *(serves 4)*

1lb/450g fresh spinach

8oz/225g courgette, sliced

8oz/225g patna rice

1 onion, peeled and finely chopped

2 garlic cloves, crushed

1 tablespoon vegan margarine

1 teaspoon black mustard seed

½ teaspoon garam masala

1 bay leaf

black pepper

20 fl.oz/600ml water

Wash the spinach, squeeze out as much water as possible and chop finely. Melt the margarine in a large pan and gently fry the onion and garlic until soft. Add the rice, mustard seed and garam masala and fry for 1 minute more, then the spinach and cook for 5 minutes while stirring. Add the water and bay leaf and season with black pepper. Stir well and bring to the boil. Cover and simmer for 10 minutes. Add the courgette and continue simmering until the liquid has been absorbed and the rice is done.

Green vegetable and lentil kedgeree   *(serves 4)*

12oz/350g prepared green vegetables (e.g. peas, green beans, green pepper, courgette, broccoli), chopped

6oz/175g green lentils

6oz/175g long grain brown rice

1 onion, peeled and finely chopped

2 garlic cloves, crushed

1oz/25g vegan margarine

1 teaspoon curry leaves

1 teaspoon cumin seed

1 teaspoon garam masala

½ teaspoon ground fenugreek

4 cloves

½ inch/1cm stick of cinnamon, crumbled

black pepper

26 fl.oz/775ml water

chopped pistachio nuts

cucumber slices

Soak the lentils in water for 2 hours, then drain and rinse well. Heat the margarine in a large pan and gently fry the onion and garlic until softened. Add the spices and fry for another minute. Stir in the lentils and rice and pour in the water. Bring to the boil, cover and simmer for 10 minutes. Add the vegetables and combine well. Bring back to the boil, then lower the heat, cover and simmer until the liquid has been absorbed and the vegetables are tender. Stir occasionally to prevent sticking, adding a little more water if necessary. Transfer to a warmed serving dish and garnish with the chopped pistachios and the cucumber slices.

Saffron rice   *(serves 4)*

8oz/225g long grain rice

½ oz/15g vegan margarine

1 onion, peeled and finely chopped

1 teaspoon yellow mustard seed

1 teaspoon saffron threads

20 fl.oz/600ml water

black pepper

Melt the margarine in a large pan and fry the onion, mustard seed and saffron until the onion is soft. Add the rice and stir around for 1 minute, then the water. Season with black pepper, stir well and bring to the boil. Cover and simmer gently until the liquid has been absorbed and the rice is cooked.

Cauliflower, mushroom and almond biryani

(serves 4)

12oz/350g cauliflower, cut into tiny florets

8oz/225g brown basmati rice

4oz/100g button mushrooms, wiped and sliced

2oz/50g flaked almonds, toasted

1oz/25g sultanas

1 onion, peeled and finely chopped

2 garlic cloves, crushed

2 tablespoons vegetable oil

1 teaspoon black mustard seed

1 teaspoon cumin seed

1 teaspoon ground coriander

1 teaspoon turmeric

¼ teaspoon chilli powder

1 inch/2.5cm stick of cinnamon, crushed

6 cardamoms, husked and the seeds separated

black pepper

30 fl.oz/900ml vegetable stock

Heat the oil in a large pan and soften the onion and garlic. Add the rice and spices and fry for 2 minutes while stirring. Add all remaining ingredients apart from the flaked almonds and stir well. Bring to the boil, cover and simmer gently until the liquid has been absorbed and the rice is tender. Remove from the heat and stir in half of the almonds. Spoon into a warmed dish and garnish with the remaining almonds before serving.

Kashmiri pilau   (*serves 4*)

8oz/225g long grain rice

8oz/225g tin pineapple rings in natural juice

4oz/100g dried apricots, chopped

1oz/25g dried dates, chopped

1oz/25g sultanas

½ oz/15g creamed coconut, grated

1 onion, peeled and finely chopped

1 inch/2.5cm piece of root ginger, peeled and finely chopped

½ oz/15g halved cashew nuts, toasted

½ oz/15g flaked almonds, toasted

1 inch/2.5cm cinnamon stick, crumbled

1 teaspoon mango powder

1 teaspoon coriander seed

½ teaspoon cumin seed

½ teaspoon fenugreek seed

½ teaspoon turmeric

4 cloves

1 tablespoon vegetable oil

Heat the oil and gently fry the onion and ginger until softened. Add the rice and spices and stir around for 2 minutes. Drain the pineapple juice into a measuring jug and make up to 20 fl.oz/600ml with water. Add the liquid to the pan, together with the apricots, dates, sultanas and coconut. Chop the pineapple rings and put in the pan. Stir well and bring to the boil. Cover and simmer gently until the liquid has been absorbed and the rice is done. Remove from the heat and stir in three-quarters of the cashews and almonds. Transfer to a warmed serving dish and garnish with the remaining nuts.

Green bean and coconut rice　　　*(serves 4)*

> 12oz/350g green beans, topped, tailed and cut into ¼ inch/5mm lengths
>
> 8oz/225g long grain brown rice
>
> 2oz/50g creamed coconut, grated
>
> 1 onion, peeled and finely chopped
>
> 1 tablespoon vegetable oil
>
> 1 teaspoon cumin seed
>
> 1 teaspoon fenugreek seed
>
> black pepper
>
> 20 fl.oz/600ml water

Fry the onion in the oil until softened. Add the rice, cumin and fenugreek seed and stir around for 1 minute, then add the water and stir well. Bring to the boil, cover and simmer for 5 minutes. Stir in the beans and coconut and season with black pepper. Bring back to the boil, cover, lower the heat and simmer until the liquid has been absorbed and the rice is tender.

Garlic and coriander rice   *(serves 4)*

8oz/225g long grain rice

4 garlic cloves, crushed

4 rounded tablespoons finely chopped fresh coriander

1 tablespoon vegetable oil

18 fl.oz/525ml water

black pepper

Heat the oil and gently fry the garlic. Add the rice and fry for 1 minute more. Add the coriander and water and season with black pepper, stir well and bring to the boil. Cover and simmer until the liquid has been absorbed and the rice is cooked.

Lemon, ginger and chickpea rice   *(serves 4)*

8oz/225g basmati rice

8oz/225g cooked chickpeas

1 lemon

1 onion, peeled and finely chopped

2 inch/5cm piece of root ginger, peeled and grated

1 tablespoon vegan margarine

20 fl.oz/600ml water

1 teaspoon yellow mustard seed

1 teaspoon curry leaves

black pepper

Cut the lemon in half, slice one half and keep for garnish. Squeeze the juice from the other half and finely grate the peel. Melt the margarine in a pan and soften the onion, ginger and lemon peel. Add the rice and mustard seed and stir around for 1 minute, then stir in the chickpeas, lemon juice, water and curry leaves. Season with black pepper and bring to the boil. Cover and simmer gently until the liquid has been absorbed and the rice is done. Put into a warmed serving dish and garnish with the lemon slices.

Mushroom and pea pilau (serves 4)

8oz/225g long grain rice

6oz/175g shelled peas

4oz/100g button mushrooms, wiped and sliced

1 onion, peeled and finely chopped

2 garlic cloves, crushed

1 tablespoon vegan margarine

1 teaspoon cumin seed

½ teaspoon turmeric

black pepper

20 fl.oz/600ml water

chopped fresh coriander leaves

Melt the margarine and fry the onion and garlic until soft. Add the rice, cumin seed and turmeric and stir around for 1 minute, then the peas, mushrooms and water. Season with black pepper, bring to the boil, cover and simmer gently until the liquid has been absorbed and the rice is tender. Serve in a warmed dish, garnished with chopped coriander leaves.

Carrot, orange and cashew nut rice   *(serves 4)*

12oz/350g carrot, scraped

8oz/225g basmati rice

1 tablespoon vegetable oil

10 fl.oz/300ml fresh orange juice

10 fl.oz/300ml water

1oz/25g sultanas

1 teaspoon coriander seed, crushed

black pepper

2oz/50g cashew nuts, toasted

1 orange, sliced

Cut the carrot into ½ inch/1cm matchsticks and gently fry in the oil for 5 minutes. Add the rice and coriander seed and stir around for another minute. Add the remaining ingredients except for the cashew nuts and sliced orange, and stir well. Bring to the boil, cover and simmer until the liquid has been absorbed and the rice is cooked. Remove from the heat and stir in half of the cashew nuts. Spoon into a warmed serving dish and garnish with the remaining nuts and the orange slices.

BREADS

In regions where wheat is readily available or rice is not grown, bread is popular and is served with meals instead of rice. Bread and rice are rarely served together at the same meal. There are many variations of Indian breads, but most are simply made with flour and water and cooked on a hot griddle or fried in oil. Naan bread is a speciality from the northern regions, where it is thrown against the walls of the tandoor to cook. All breads should be freshly made for each meal and served hot. To keep the bread warm while cooking the next one, wrap in foil and place in a moderate oven until ready to serve.

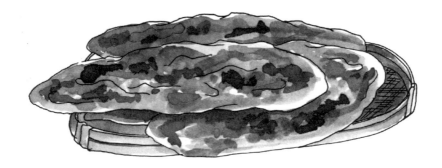

Chapatis   *(makes 12)*

8oz/225g plain wholewheat flour
½ teaspoon salt
water

Mix the flour with the salt and stir in enough water to form a stiff dough. Knead well, then cover and chill for 1 hour. Knead the dough again and divide it into 12 equal portions. Form the portions into balls and roll out each ball on a floured surface into a circle of about 5 inches/13cm. Heat a heavy-based frying pan until hot and cook the chapatis for about a minute on each side until lightly browned.

Parathas   *(makes 12)*

8oz/225g plain wholewheat flour
½ teaspoon salt
water
melted vegan margarine

Mix the flour with the salt and add enough water to make a stiff dough. Knead well, cover and chill for an hour, then knead the dough again and divide it into 12 equal pieces. Roll each piece of dough into a ball, then roll these out on a floured surface to form a circle of about 5 inches/13cm. Brush each circle with melted margarine and fold in half, then brush again with melted margarine and fold in half. Roll out the resulting triangles lightly and fry them in a little margarine in a heavy-based pan for about 1 minute. Brush the top with margarine, turn over and cook until golden brown.

Naan   *(makes 4)*

1lb/450g plain flour

1 teaspoon salt

1 dessertspoon easy-blend yeast

2 tablespoons melted vegan margarine or vegetable oil

5 fl.oz/150ml plain soya yoghurt

approx. 5 fl.oz/150ml warm water

extra melted vegan margarine

onion seeds

sesame seeds

Put the flour, salt and yeast in a mixing bowl and combine. Add the 2 tablespoonfuls of melted margarine or oil and the yoghurt. Gradually add the water until a soft dough forms. Knead well, then return to the bowl, cover and leave in a warm place for 1 hour to rise. Knead the dough again and divide it into 4 equal pieces. Stretch or roll each piece of dough into a pear shape. Brush the tops with melted margarine and sprinkle with onion and sesame seeds. Bake in a preheated oven at 200°C/400°F/Gas mark 6 for 10-12 minutes until golden.

Rich naan   *(makes 4)*

1oz/25g desiccated coconut

1oz/25g sultanas

½ oz/15g flaked almonds

1 teaspoon cumin seed

Add to the dry naan ingredients and proceed as above.

Puri   *(makes 16)*

8oz/225g plain wholemeal flour

pinch of salt

¼ teaspoon chilli powder

water

vegetable oil

Sieve the flour, salt and chilli powder into a bowl and mix in enough water to form a soft dough. Knead well and leave for 10 minutes. Divide the dough into 16 equal portions and roll out each one into a small circle of 3 inches/7.5cm. Fry the puris in hot oil for a minute or so on each side until browned and risen. Drain on kitchen paper.

Stuffed puri   *(makes 12)*

12oz/350g plain wholemeal flour

pinch of salt

¼ teaspoon ground chilli powder

water

vegetable oil

filling

1 onion, peeled

2 garlic cloves

½ inch/1cm piece of root ginger, peeled

1 rounded teaspoon cumin seed

1 rounded teaspoon ground coriander

½ teaspoon turmeric

black pepper

Sieve the flour, salt and chilli powder into a large bowl and add enough water to mix to a soft dough. Knead well and leave for 10 minutes. Mince the onion with the garlic and ginger, add the spices and mix very well. Divide the dough into 12 equal pieces and roll or shape each piece into a flat round of about 3 inches/7.5cm. Divide the filling equally between the rounds, then fold the pastry over to enclose the filling. Form each parcel into a ball and roll or shape these into ovals. Fry the puris in hot oil for a minute or so on each side until golden and risen. Drain them on kitchen paper before serving.

MAIN COURSES

Layered dishes containing grains and vegetables and casserole-style meals are examples of recipes which are thought to have originated in Gujarat but are now popular throughout the country. The Islamic custom of serving vegetables stuffed with spicy mixtures is prevalent in the Hyderabad region, where many Muslims live. Suggested accompaniments are given for each recipe, to provide filling main course meals.

Spiced vegetable and almond casserole (serves 4)

8oz/225g carrot, scraped and chopped

8oz/225g green beans, topped, tailed and cut into 1 inch/2.5cm lengths

8oz/225g button mushrooms, wiped and halved

4oz/100g red pepper, chopped

2oz/50g small natural textured vegetable protein chunks

2oz/50g dried apricots, chopped

1 onion, peeled and chopped

2 garlic cloves, crushed

1 tablespoon vegetable oil

1 rounded dessertspoon gram flour

1 rounded teaspoon ground coriander

1 rounded teaspoon ground cumin

1 rounded teaspoon black mustard seed

½ teaspoon ground cinnamon

½ teaspoon turmeric

½ teaspoon ground fenugreek

black pepper

32 fl.oz/950ml vegetable stock

3oz/75g ground almonds

toasted flaked almonds

Heat the oil in a large pan and gently fry the onion and garlic until softened. Add the coriander, cumin, mustard seed, cinnamon, turmeric and fenugreek and stir around for 30 seconds. Dissolve the gram flour in a little of the stock and set aside. Add the remaining stock to the pan together with the vegetable protein and bring to the boil. Remove from the heat, cover and leave for 1 hour. Add the vegetables and apricots and season with black pepper. Stir well, bring to the boil, cover and simmer for 3 minutes. Stir in the dissolved gram flour and the ground almonds and simmer for a further minute. Transfer to a casserole dish, cover and bake in a preheated oven at 180°C/350°F/Gas mark 4 for 40 minutes. Garnish with toasted flaked almonds and serve with plain boiled rice.

Okra and peanut hotpot   *(serves 4)*

base

1lb/450g okra, topped and tailed

8oz/225g tomatoes, skinned and chopped

2oz/50g small natural textured vegetable protein chunks

1oz/25g sultanas

1 onion, peeled and chopped

16 fl.oz/475ml vegetable stock

2 rounded tablespoons smooth peanut butter

1 tablespoon vegetable oil

2 rounded teaspoons curry powder

1 teaspoon cumin seed

1 teaspoon fenugreek seed

½ teaspoon turmeric

a few curry leaves

black pepper

topping

2lb/900g potatoes, peeled and thinly sliced

1oz/25g shelled roasted peanuts, finely chopped

vegetable oil

garam masala

Soak the vegetable protein in the stock for an hour. Fry the onion in the oil until soft, add the curry powder, cumin and fenugreek seed and turmeric and stir around for 30 seconds, then the tomatoes and fry until pulpy. Strain the vegetable stock into the pan, add the peanut butter and stir until it dissolves. Put the vegetable protein chunks, sultanas and curry leaves in, together with the okra, cut into ¾ inch/2cm diagonal slices. Season with black pepper and stir well. Bring to the boil, cover and simmer gently for 15 minutes, then transfer to a casserole dish.

Boil the potato slices for 5 minutes, drain and arrange evenly over the vegetables. Brush the top with oil and sprinkle with the chopped peanuts and garam masala. Cover and bake in a preheated oven at 180°C/350°F/Gas mark 4 for 25 minutes. Uncover and bake for a further 5 minutes until golden brown. Serve with bread and a salad.

Cauliflower and chickpea korma and garlic rice
(serves 4)

base

8oz/225g long grain brown rice

1 tablespoon vegetable oil

3 garlic cloves, crushed

20 fl.oz/600ml water

½ teaspoon turmeric

black pepper

filling

1lb/450g cauliflower, cut into small florets

8oz/225g cooked chickpeas

1oz/25g sultanas

1 onion, peeled and finely chopped

1 garlic clove, crushed

14 fl.oz/400ml water

4 fl.oz/125ml soya milk

1 tablespoon vegetable oil

2 rounded dessertspoons korma curry paste

2 dessertspoons cornflour

4 cardamoms, husked and the seeds separated

black pepper

2 rounded tablespoons plain soya yoghurt

topping

2oz/50g flaked almonds, chopped

garam masala

Heat the oil for the base layer and soften the garlic. Add the rice and turmeric and stir around for 1 minute. Stir in the water and season with black pepper. Bring to the boil, cover and simmer gently until the liquid has been absorbed and the rice is cooked. Spoon the rice into a shallow greased casserole dish and press it down evenly with the back of a spoon.

Heat the oil for the filling and gently fry the onion and garlic until softened. Add the curry paste and stir around for 30 seconds. Stir in the cauliflower, sultanas, water and cardamoms and season with black pepper. Bring to the boil, cover and simmer for about 10 minutes until the cauliflower is just tender. Dissolve the cornflour in the soya milk and add to the pan together with the chickpeas. Raise the heat and stir until the sauce thickens. Remove from the heat and stir in the yoghurt. Spoon the mixture evenly over the rice layer and sprinkle the chopped almonds and a little garam masala on top. Cover and bake in a preheated oven at 180°C/350°F/Gas mark 4 for 30 minutes. Serve with a vegetable accompaniment.

Spiced millet and spinach (serves 4)

millet layer
8oz/225g millet

8oz/225g carrot, scraped and grated

2 tablespoons vegetable oil

1 rounded teaspoon yellow mustard seed

1 rounded teaspoon cumin seed

½ teaspoon turmeric

20 fl.oz/600ml water

spinach layer
1lb/450g fresh spinach

8oz/225g courgette, chopped

8oz/225g green beans, topped, tailed and chopped

1 onion, peeled and finely chopped

2 garlic cloves, crushed

2 tablespoons vegetable oil

1 rounded teaspoon garam masala

1 rounded teaspoon black mustard seed

½ teaspoon fenugreek

pinch of chilli powder

6 cardamoms, husked and the seeds separated

black pepper

4 fl.oz/125ml soya milk

1 rounded dessertspoon cornflour

topping

1oz/25g pistachio nuts, grated

2 tomatoes, sliced

chopped fresh coriander leaves

Heat the oil for the millet layer and fry the carrot, cumin and mustard seed and turmeric for 2 minutes. Stir in the millet and water and bring to the boil. Cover and simmer gently, stirring occasionally, until the liquid has been absorbed and the millet is done. Spoon the mixture into a shallow greased baking dish and press it down evenly.

Wash the spinach, squeeze out excess water and chop finely. Heat the oil in a large pan and gently fry the onion and garlic until soft. Add the garam masala, mustard seed, fenugreek, chilli powder and cardamoms and fry for 30 seconds more. Stir in the spinach, courgette and green beans and season with black pepper. Cook for about 10 minutes until just tender. Mix the cornflour with the soya milk and add to the pan. Raise the heat and stir until the mixture thickens. Spoon the spinach mixture evenly over the millet. Sprinkle the pistachios on top and finish with the tomato slices. Cover and bake in a preheated oven at 180°C/350°F/Gas mark 4 for 25 minute. Garnish with chopped fresh coriander and serve with a vegetable dish.

Spiced stuffed aubergines   (serves 4)

2 aubergines (each approx. 12oz/350g)

6oz/175g mushrooms, wiped and finely chopped

2oz/50g ground almonds

1oz/25g natural minced textured vegetable protein

8 fl.oz/225ml vegetable stock

1 onion, peeled and finely chopped

2 garlic cloves, crushed

4 tablespoons vegetable oil

1 rounded teaspoon garam masala

1 rounded teaspoon black mustard seed

1 rounded teaspoon cumin seed

1 rounded teaspoon fenugreek seed

black pepper

flaked almonds

extra vegetable oil

Cut the aubergines in half lengthwise and remove the flesh, leaving the shells approximately ¼ inch/5mm thick. Brush the shells inside and out with oil and put them in a shallow baking dish.

Soak the vegetable protein in the stock for 15 minutes. Chop the aubergine flesh finely and fry with the onion and garlic in the oil for 10 minutes, stirring frequently. Add the garam masala, mustard, cumin and fenugreek seed and mushrooms and fry for 2 minutes more, then add the soaked vegetable protein and remaining stock and season with black pepper. Bring to the boil and simmer for 5 minutes, stirring occasionally. Remove from the heat and add the ground almonds. Mix thoroughly, then divide the mixture between the 4 aubergine shells and sprinkle the tops with flaked almonds. Cover and bake in a preheated oven at 180°C/350°F/Gas mark 4 for 40 minutes. Uncover and bake for another 5 minutes until browned. Serve with a savoury rice dish.

Stuffed cabbage leaves with peanut and ginger sauce *(serves 4)*

16 large cabbage leaves

6 fl.oz/175ml vegetable stock

filling

6oz/175g long grain rice

2oz/50g red pepper, finely chopped

2oz/50g mushrooms, wiped and finely chopped

2oz/50g sweetcorn kernels

2oz/50g tomato, skinned and chopped

1 onion, peeled and finely chopped

2 garlic cloves, crushed

½ green chilli, finely chopped

1 tablespoon vegetable oil

1 teaspoon tamarind purée

1 teaspoon cumin seed

¼ teaspoon turmeric

¼ teaspoon ground fenugreek

black pepper

12 fl.oz/350ml water

sauce

1 onion, peeled and chopped

1 inch/2.5cm piece of root ginger, peeled and chopped

2 rounded tablespoons peanut butter

4 fl.oz/125ml water

1 dessertspoon vegetable oil

½ teaspoon ground cumin

½ teaspoon paprika

black pepper

2 rounded tablespoons plain soya yoghurt

Heat the oil for the filling in a large pan and gently fry the onion, garlic and chilli until soft. Add the rice, cumin seed, turmeric and fenugreek and fry for another 2 minutes. Put in the remaining filling ingredients and stir well. Bring to the boil, cover and simmer until the liquid has been absorbed and the rice is cooked. Remove from the heat and allow to cool.

Blanch the cabbage leaves in a large pan of boiling water for 3 minutes. Drain the leaves and allow them to cool, then cut out the thick stalks. Divide the filling between the leaves, placing it neatly in the centre. Fold each leaf around the filling to make little parcels. Put the stuffed leaves with the joins underneath in a lightly oiled shallow baking dish and pour the stock over. Cover and bake in a preheated oven at 180°C/350°F/Gas mark 4 for 30 minutes.

Meanwhile, make the sauce. Blend the onion with the ginger until smooth and fry in the oil until golden. Add the cumin and paprika and fry for 30 seconds more, then remove from the heat and add the remaining sauce ingredients. Mix together until smooth. Return to the heat and cook gently whilst stirring until hot. Pour the sauce over the baked stuffed cabbage leaves and serve with bread and a vegetable or salad dish.

Stuffed marrow rings   *(serves 4)*

8 marrow slices (approx. 1¼ inch/3.25cm thick)

1 red onion, peeled and finely chopped

2 garlic cloves, crushed

1 inch/2.5cm piece of root ginger, peeled and finely chopped

2oz/50g natural minced textured vegetable protein

4oz/50g red pepper, finely chopped

4oz/100g tomato, skinned and chopped

1 tablespoon vegetable oil

1oz/25g cashew nuts, grated

10 fl.oz/300ml vegetable stock

1 teaspoon curry powder

1 teaspoon cumin seed

½ teaspoon paprika

black pepper

garam masala

Heat the oil and gently fry the onion, garlic, ginger and red pepper until soft. Add the curry powder, paprika and cumin seed and stir around for 1 minute. Now add the vegetable protein, tomato and stock and season with black pepper. Combine well and bring to the boil. Cover and simmer for 10 minutes, stirring occasionally, until the liquid has been absorbed. Remove from the heat and stir in the grated cashews.

Cut the pulpy centres out of the marrow slices. Put the rings in an oiled baking dish and brush the tops with oil. Divide the filling between the marrow rings and sprinkle the top with garam masala. Cover and bake in a preheated oven at 180°C/350°F/Gas mark 4 for about 45 minutes until the marrow is just tender. Serve with a savoury rice dish.

Stuffed peppers with spicy tomato sauce *(serves 4)*

4 large peppers

chopped fresh coriander leaves

filling

8oz/225g long grain rice

4oz/100g sweetcorn kernels

4oz/100g shelled peas

1 onion, peeled and finely chopped

2 garlic cloves, crushed

1 inch/2.5cm piece of root ginger, peeled and finely chopped

1 tablespoon vegetable oil

20 fl.oz/600ml water

1 dessertspoon dried lemon grass

1 teaspoon yellow mustard seed

½ teaspoon turmeric

black pepper

sauce

14oz/400g tin chopped tomatoes

1 small green chilli, finely chopped

2 garlic cloves, crushed

1 dessertspoon vegetable oil

1 dessertspoon tamarind purée

1 teaspoon ground cumin

black pepper

Cut the peppers in half lengthwise and remove the stalks, membranes and seeds, then blanch the halves for 2 minutes in a large pan of boiling water. Drain and arrange the peppers in an oiled baking dish.

Heat the oil for the filling and soften the onion, garlic and ginger. Add the rice, lemon grass, mustard seed and turmeric and stir around for 1 minute, then the sweetcorn, peas and water. Season with black pepper, stir well and bring to the boil. Cover and simmer gently until the liquid has been absorbed and the rice is done. Spoon the mixture into the pepper halves.

Fry the chilli and garlic in the oil for the sauce until soft. Add the cumin and stir around for 30 seconds. Now add the tomatoes and tamarind and season with black pepper. Raise the heat and simmer for 10 minutes, stirring occasionally. Spoon the sauce over the filled peppers and cover the dish loosely with foil. Bake in a preheated oven at 180°C/350°F/Gas mark 4 for about 30 minutes until the peppers are tender. Garnish with chopped fresh coriander leaves and serve with bread and a salad accompaniment.

Curried vegetable and fruit pie   *(serves 4)*

pastry

6oz/175g fine wholemeal self raising flour

2½oz/60g vegan margarine

1 teaspoon garam masala

water

soya milk

black onion seeds

filling

2lb/900g root vegetables, peeled and diced

2 eating apples, peeled, cored and diced

2oz/50g dried apricots, chopped

1oz/25g sultanas

2oz/50g small natural textured vegetable protein chunks

1 onion, peeled and chopped

2 garlic cloves, crushed

1 inch/2.5cm piece of root ginger, peeled and grated

1oz/25g creamed coconut, grated

1 tablespoon vegetable oil

30 fl.oz/900ml vegetable stock

2 rounded teaspoons ground cumin

1 teaspoon fenugreek seed

1 teaspoon coriander seed, slightly crushed

1 teaspoon turmeric

½ teaspoon mango powder

1 inch/2.5cm cinnamon stick, crushed

black pepper

Heat the oil in a large pan and gently fry the onion, garlic and ginger until softened. Add the cumin, fenugreek and coriander seed, turmeric, mango powder and cinnamon stick and stir around for 30 seconds. Add 20 fl.oz/600ml of the vegetable stock and the vegetable protein and season with black pepper. Bring to the boil, cover and remove from the heat, and leave for 30 minutes. Then add the diced vegetables, apple, apricots and sultanas, together with the remaining stock. Stir well and bring to the boil. Cover and simmer for about 20 minutes until the stock has been absorbed and the vegetables are just done. Add the coconut and stir until it dissolves. Transfer the mixture to a deep baking dish.

Sift the garam masala with the flour, rub in the margarine and add enough water to bind. Knead well. Turn the dough out onto a floured board and roll it out to fit the top of the baking dish. Place the pastry over the vegetable and fruit mixture and decorate the edges with a fork. Prick the top all over and brush with soya milk. Sprinkle with onion seeds and bake in a preheated oven at 180°C/350°F/Gas mark 4 for about 30 minutes until golden. Serve with saffron rice (see page 49).

Aubergine, rice and nut balls in lentil and carrot sauce *(serves 4)*

nut balls

12oz/350g aubergine, finely chopped

1 red onion, peeled and finely chopped

2 garlic cloves, crushed

4oz/100g long grain rice

4oz/100g mixed nuts, ground

2oz/50g ground rice

1oz/25g gram flour

3 tablespoons vegetable oil

1 rounded teaspoon ground coriander

1 rounded teaspoon ground cumin

½ teaspoon mango powder

¼ teaspoon ground cinnamon

black pepper

extra vegetable oil

sauce

4oz/100g carrot, scraped and grated

4oz/100g tomatoes, skinned and chopped

3oz/75g red lentils

1 onion, peeled and finely chopped

1 garlic clove, crushed

1 small red chilli, finely chopped

1 tablespoon vegetable oil

1 rounded teaspoon cumin seed

1 teaspoon yellow mustard seed

½ teaspoon paprika

½ teaspoon turmeric

black pepper

10 fl.oz/300ml vegetable stock

chopped fresh coriander leaves

First make the nut balls. Cook the rice until tender, drain thoroughly and set aside. Heat the oil and gently fry the aubergine, onion and garlic for about 15 minutes until soft, stirring frequently to prevent sticking. Add the coriander, cumin, mango powder and cinnamon and stir around for 30 seconds. Remove from the heat and stir in the cooked rice and remaining nut ball ingredients. Mix thoroughly, cover and chill for 1 hour.

Heat the oil for the sauce and soften the carrot, onion, garlic and chilli for 5 minutes. Add the cumin and mustard seed, paprika and turmeric and stir around for another 30 seconds. Wash and drain the lentils and add to the pan, together with the tomato and stock. Season with black pepper and stir well. Bring to the boil, cover and simmer gently for 30 minutes, stirring occasionally.

Take rounded tablespoonfuls of the nut mixture and roll into balls in the palm of the hand. Brush the balls with vegetable oil and put them in a lightly oiled ovenproof dish. Bake in a preheated oven at 180°C/350°F/Gas mark 4 for 30 minutes.

Pour the hot sauce over the nut balls and garnish with chopped fresh coriander leaves. Serve with a savoury rice dish or with bread and a salad.

Vegetable kebabs   *(serves 4)*

2lb/900g mixed prepared vegetables (choose from aubergine,
      courgette, mushroom, tomato, onion, peppers)

marinade

1 red onion, peeled and chopped

2 garlic cloves, chopped

1 small red chilli, chopped

1 inch/2.5cm piece of root ginger, peeled and chopped

2 tablespoons vegetable oil

2 tablespoons lemon juice

½ teaspoon turmeric

½ teaspoon mango powder

1 rounded teaspoon ground cumin

2 rounded teaspoons ground coriander

black pepper

Put all the marinade ingredients in a blender and blend until smooth. Cut the vegetables into even-sized chunks and put them in a large bowl. Add the marinade and mix very well. Cover and leave for at least 4 hours.

Thread the coated vegetables onto small square skewers and place them under a hot grill for about 20 minutes, turning occasionally, until just tender. Serve on a bed of savoury rice.

Potato, carrot and lentil Madras   *(serves 4)*

1lb/450g new potatoes, scraped and diced

1lb/450g carrots, scraped and diced

4oz/100g red lentils

14oz/400g tin crushed tomatoes

1 onion, peeled and finely chopped

1 small red chilli, finely chopped

1 tablespoon vegetable oil

1 tablespoon tomato purée

2 rounded teaspoons Madras curry powder

1 teaspoon ground coriander

½ teaspoon cumin seed

½ teaspoon paprika

black pepper

chopped fresh coriander leaves

Boil the lentils for 5 minutes, then drain and keep the cooking water. Boil the potato and carrot for 5 minutes and drain. Heat the oil in a large pan and gently fry the onion and chilli until soft. Add the curry powder, coriander, cumin seed and paprika and fry for another 30 seconds. Add the lentils, potato, carrot, crushed tomatoes and tomato purée and 8 fl.oz/225ml of the lentil water. Season with black pepper and stir well. Bring to the boil, cover and simmer gently for 20-25 minutes until cooked, stirring frequently to prevent sticking. Add a little more lentil water if necessary. Garnish with chopped coriander leaves and serve with a savoury rice dish.

Sweet potato, butter bean and peanut curry
(serves 4)

1½lb/675g sweet potato, peeled and diced

12oz/350g cooked butter beans

1oz/25g dried dates, finely chopped

1 onion, peeled and finely chopped

1 tablespoon vegetable oil

1 rounded tablespoon peanut butter

10 fl.oz/300ml coconut milk

10 fl.oz/300ml water

1 rounded teaspoon ground cumin

1 rounded teaspoon ground coriander

1 teaspoon mango powder

½ teaspoon paprika

½ teaspoon turmeric

black pepper

2oz/50g roasted peanuts, chopped and toasted

Fry the onion in the oil in a large pan until soft. Add the cumin, coriander, mango powder, paprika and turmeric and stir around for 30 seconds. Put in the coconut milk, water and peanut butter and stir until the butter dissolves. Now add the sweet potato and dates and season with black pepper. Bring to the boil, cover and simmer gently for about 20 minutes until the potato is just done, stirring frequently to prevent sticking. Add the butter beans and continue simmering, while stirring, for a further 2 minutes. Garnish with the chopped peanuts and serve with a savoury rice dish.

THALI AND SIDE DISHES

The following vegetable, fruit, nut and pulse dishes are all suitable for serving as part of a thali-style meal. A couple of these dishes, served with dhal, raita, chutney and rice or bread, will provide a filling main course meal for four people. To serve two people simply choose one of the recipes and add a savoury rice dish to provide a quick main course. Indian vegetables are always lightly spiced and cooked dry, with a touch of added liquid, or more elaborately in a sauce.

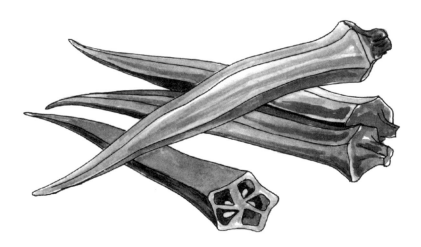

Dry spiced potato   *(serves 4)*

1½lb/675g evenly-sized new potatoes, scraped

1 onion, peeled and chopped

1 garlic clove

2 tablespoons vegetable oil

1 teaspoon black mustard seed

½ teaspoon turmeric

¼ teaspoon chilli powder

black pepper

a little water

chopped fresh coriander leaves

Boil the potatoes until just cooked, drain and dice. Blend the onion and garlic to a paste. Dry roast the mustard seed in a heavy-based pan until they pop. Add the oil and onion and garlic paste and fry until lightly golden, then the turmeric and chilli powder and stir around for 30 seconds more. Now add the diced potatoes and two tablespoonfuls of water. Season with black pepper and stir well. Continue cooking for a couple of minutes until the potatoes are heated through. Garnish with chopped coriander leaves.

Hot spicy corn with peppers   *(serves 4)*

12oz/350g sweetcorn kernels

12oz/350g tomatoes, skinned and chopped

3oz/75g red pepper, chopped

3oz/75g orange pepper, chopped

1 green chilli, finely chopped

1 onion, peeled and finely chopped

2 garlic cloves, crushed

1 tablespoon vegetable oil

1 dessertspoon tamarind purée

1 rounded teaspoon garam masala

1 rounded teaspoon ground coriander

½ teaspoon turmeric

a few curry leaves

finely sliced spring onions

Heat the oil and fry the onion, garlic, chilli and peppers until softened. Add the spices and stir around for 30 seconds, then add the tomatoes and cook gently until pulpy. Stir in the tamarind purée and the sweetcorn and simmer for 10 minutes, stirring occasionally to prevent sticking. Serve garnished with sliced spring onions.

Mushroom masala (serves 4)

1lb/450g button mushrooms, wiped and halved

1 onion, peeled and chopped

2 garlic cloves

2 tablespoons vegetable oil

1 teaspoon garam masala

2 rounded tablespoons plain soya yoghurt

chopped fresh coriander leaves

Blend the onion with the garlic, then fry in the oil until golden. Add the garam masala and mushrooms and fry until the juices begin to run. Stir in the yoghurt and raise the heat until heated through. Garnish with chopped fresh coriander.

Sweet potato with coconut (*serves 4*)

1½lb/675g sweet potato, peeled and diced

1 onion, peeled and chopped

2 tablespoons vegetable oil

1oz/25g creamed coconut, grated

4 fl.oz/125ml water

1 teaspoon yellow mustard seed

1 teaspoon cumin seed

1 teaspoon garam masala

1 teaspoon turmeric

Boil the potatoes until just tender and drain. Blend the onion to a paste, then fry this in the oil until golden. Add the spices and stir around for 30 seconds. Now put in the coconut and water and heat gently whilst stirring until the coconut dissolves. Add the drained potato and continue stirring until heated through.

Spiced aubergine with peppers (*serves 4*)

12oz/350g aubergine, diced

4oz/100g green pepper, sliced

4oz/100g red pepper, sliced

1 large eating apple, peeled, cored and diced

1oz/25g sultanas

½ inch/1cm piece of root ginger, peeled and finely chopped

1 onion, peeled and finely chopped

2 garlic cloves, crushed

4 tablespoons vegetable oil

12 fl.oz/350ml water

2 rounded teaspoons ground cumin

1 rounded teaspoon turmeric

½ teaspoon ground cinnamon

4 cardamoms, husked and the seeds separated

1 rounded tablespoon plain soya yoghurt

thin red chilli rings

Fry the aubergine, onion, garlic and ginger in the oil in a large saucepan for 10 minutes, stirring frequently to prevent sticking. Add the spices and stir around for 30 seconds more, then stir in the red and green pepper, apple, sultanas and water and bring to the boil. Cover and simmer gently for about 25 minutes, stirring occasionally, until the liquid has been absorbed and the vegetables are tender. Add the yoghurt and continue cooking for a couple of minutes. Garnish with thin red chilli rings when serving.

Potatoes with spinach   *(serves 4)*

1½lb/675g potatoes, scraped and diced

12oz/350g fresh spinach, trimmed and chopped

2 tablespoons vegetable oil

1 onion, peeled and chopped

2 garlic cloves

1 teaspoon garam masala

Blend the onion with the garlic and fry in the oil until golden. Then add the potatoes and garam masala and fry for 5 minutes. Put in the spinach, cover and cook for 20-25 minutes until done, stirring frequently to prevent sticking.

Dry spiced parsnip   *(serves 4)*

1½lb/675g parsnip, peeled and diced

1 onion, peeled and finely chopped

1 tablespoon vegetable oil

1 teaspoon yellow mustard seed

1 teaspoon ground coriander

½ teaspoon ground ginger

pinch of chilli powder

Boil the parsnip until just tender and drain. Heat the oil and gently soften the onion. Add the mustard seed, coriander, ginger and chilli powder and stir around for 30 seconds. Add the parsnip and continue cooking for a couple of minutes until heated through.

Green beans with coconut   *(serves 4)*

1lb/450g green beans, topped, tailed and cut into 1 inch/2.5cm lengths

1 onion, peeled and chopped

2 garlic cloves

1 inch/2.5cm piece of root ginger, peeled

1oz/25g creamed coconut, grated

1 tablespoon vegetable oil

1 teaspoon garam masala

1 teaspoon yellow mustard seed

½ teaspoon turmeric

4 fl.oz/125ml water

toasted flaked coconut

Blend the onion with the garlic and ginger and fry in the oil for 10 minutes. Add the spices and fry for 30 seconds more, then put in the beans and water and bring to the boil. Simmer until the beans are just done, adding a little more water if necessary to prevent sticking. Stir in the creamed coconut and continue cooking until it dissolves. Garnish with toasted flaked coconut.

Garlic potatoes   *(serves 4)*

1¼lb/550g potatoes, scraped

2 large garlic cloves, crushed

1 small red chilli, finely chopped

2 tablespoons vegetable oil

½ teaspoon turmeric

½ teaspoon black mustard seed

black pepper

Cut the potatoes into 1 inch/2.5cm long matchsticks. Wash and dry thoroughly on kitchen paper. Heat the oil in a heavy-based pan and gently fry the garlic, chilli, turmeric and mustard seed for 1 minute. Add the potatoes and fry for 10-15 minutes, turning frequently, until golden. Season with black pepper and serve.

Spiced cabbage and sultana sauté   *(serves 4)*

12oz/350g white cabbage, finely shredded

2oz/50g sultanas

4 fl.oz/125ml water

1 tablespoon vegetable oil

1 teaspoon cumin seed

1 teaspoon garam masala

1 teaspoon ground coriander

In a large pan gently fry the spices for 1 minute in the oil. Add the cabbage and fry for 3 minutes while stirring. Add the sultanas and water and raise the heat. Cook for a few minutes, until the cabbage is just tender. Add a little more water if necessary and stir frequently to prevent sticking.

Spinach with tomatoes *(serves 4)*

1lb/450g fresh spinach, trimmed and chopped

6oz/175g tomatoes, skinned and chopped

1oz/25g vegan margarine

1 onion, peeled and finely chopped

1 small green chilli, finely chopped

1 garlic clove, crushed

1 teaspoon tamarind purée

1 teaspoon cumin seed

1 teaspoon black mustard seed

¼ teaspoon grated nutmeg

Melt the margarine in a large pan and gently fry the onion, chilli and garlic until soft. Add the spices and stir around for 30 seconds. Add the spinach and combine well. Cover and cook for 5 minutes. Now stir in the tomatoes and tamarind purée. Continue cooking for 10 minutes until done, stirring frequently to prevent sticking.

Aubergine with brown lentils and fruit *(serves 4)*

10oz/300g aubergine, finely chopped

2oz/50g brown lentils

1oz/25g dried dates, finely chopped

1oz/25g dried apricots, finely chopped

1oz/25g sultanas

1 eating apple, peeled, cored and finely chopped

1 celery stick, trimmed and finely sliced

1 onion, peeled and finely chopped

1 garlic clove, crushed

3 tablespoons vegetable oil

1 teaspoon cumin seed

½ teaspoon coriander seed

¼ teaspoon ground cinnamon

15 fl.oz/450ml water

garam masala

Soak the lentils in water for 1 hour, drain and bring to the boil in a fresh pan of water. Cover and simmer briskly for 15 minutes, then drain again. Heat the oil in a large pan and fry the aubergine, onion, garlic and celery for 10 minutes, stirring frequently to prevent sticking. Add the cumin and coriander seed and the cinnamon and stir around for 30 seconds. Add the lentils, fruit and water and bring to the boil. Cover and simmer for about 40 minutes, until the liquid has been absorbed and the mixture is thick, stirring frequently. Garnish with garam masala.

Potatoes with tomato *(serves 4)*

1½lb/675g potatoes, scraped and diced

6oz/175g tomatoes, skinned and chopped

1 onion, peeled and chopped

1 garlic clove, crushed

1 tablespoon vegetable oil

1 dessertspoon tamarind purée

1 teaspoon black mustard seed

½ teaspoon paprika

black pepper

3 fl.oz/75ml water

chopped fresh basil

Blend the onion with the garlic and fry in the oil for 5 minutes. Add the mustard seed and paprika and stir around for 30 seconds, then the potatoes and water and season with black pepper. Stir well and cook for 10 minutes, stirring frequently. Now add the tomatoes and tamarind and cook for 12-15 minutes more until the potatoes are done, stirring regularly to prevent sticking. Serve garnished with chopped fresh basil.

Broccoli and mushrooms in creamy almond sauce
(serves 4)

12oz/350g broccoli, cut into small florets

4oz/100g button mushrooms, wiped and halved

1 onion, peeled and finely chopped

2 garlic cloves, crushed

2oz/50g ground almonds

1oz/25g flaked almonds, toasted

1 tablespoon vegetable oil

1 dessertspoon mild curry paste

1 teaspoon black mustard seed

½ teaspoon ground mace

black pepper

10 fl.oz/300ml water

4 fl.oz/125ml soya milk

1 dessertspoon cornflour

Heat the oil and gently fry the onion and garlic until softened. Add the curry paste, mustard seed and mace and stir around for 30 seconds. Then put in the broccoli, mushrooms and water and season with black pepper, stir well and bring to the boil. Cover and simmer gently until the vegetables are just tender. Dissolve the cornflour in the soya milk and add to the pan together with the ground almonds. Combine well and, stirring all the while, bring back to the boil and cook for a minute or two until the sauce thickens. Remove from the heat and stir in half of the flaked almonds. Serve garnished with the remaining almonds.

Bengali vegetables with chickpeas   *(serves 4)*

1¼lb/550g prepared vegetables of your choice, chopped

4oz/100g cooked chickpeas

1 onion, peeled and finely chopped

1 tablespoon vegetable oil

6 tablespoons water

2 rounded tablespoons plain soya yoghurt

2 teaspoons panchphoran

½ teaspoon mango powder

black pepper

chopped fresh coriander leaves

Gently fry the panchphoran in the oil for 15 seconds. Add the onion and fry until soft, then the turmeric and mango powder and stir around for a few seconds. Add the vegetables and water and season with black pepper. Cook gently until the vegetables are just tender and the mixture is dry, adding a little more water if necessary to prevent sticking. Stir in the chickpeas and yoghurt and continue cooking for a couple of minutes until heated through. Garnish with chopped fresh coriander to serve.

Soya mince and pea curry   *(serves 4)*

8oz/225g frozen peas

6oz/175g tomatoes, skinned and chopped

2oz/50g natural minced textured vegetable protein

1 red onion, peeled and finely chopped

2 garlic cloves, crushed

1 small red chilli, finely chopped

8 fl.oz/225ml vegetable stock

1 tablespoon vegetable oil

1 dessertspoon tomato purée

1 rounded teaspoon cumin seed

1 rounded teaspoon curry powder

½ teaspoon turmeric

¼ teaspoon ground cinnamon

6 cardamoms, husked and the seeds separated

black pepper

chopped fresh coriander leaves

Heat the oil in a pan and fry the onion, garlic and chilli until soft. Add the cumin seed, curry powder, turmeric, cinnamon and cardamom seeds and fry for another 30 seconds. Remove from the heat and stir in the vegetable protein, stock and tomato purée. Cover and leave for 10 minutes, then add the peas and tomatoes and season with black pepper. Return to the heat and bring to the boil. Simmer for 10-15 minutes, stirring frequently, until the mixture thickens. Use chopped fresh coriander as garnish.

Okra with tomato and peanut sauce   *(serves 4)*

1¼lb/550g okra, topped, tailed and cut into diagonal chunks

1lb/450g tomatoes, skinned and chopped

1 onion, peeled and chopped

2 garlic cloves

3 tablespoons vegetable oil

1 rounded tablespoon peanut butter

1 teaspoon yellow mustard seed

1 teaspoon cumin seed

½ teaspoon turmeric

½ teaspoon ground fenugreek

black pepper

shelled chopped peanuts

Blend the onion with the garlic and gently fry it with the okra in the oil for 10 minutes. Add the mustard and cumin seed, turmeric and fenugreek and stir around for 30 seconds. Now add the tomatoes and simmer, stirring occasionally, for about 5 minutes until the okra is just done and the sauce thickens. Add the peanut butter and season with black pepper. Simmer for another minute or two, then garnish with the chopped peanuts and serve.

Spiced cauliflower with cashews   *(serves 4)*

1 lb/450g cauliflower, cut into small florets

1 onion, peeled and chopped

2 garlic cloves, crushed

3oz/75g cashew nuts, ground

1oz/25g sultanas

1 tablespoon sunflower oil

12 fl.oz/350ml water

1 rounded teaspoon ground cumin

1 rounded teaspoon ground coriander

1 rounded teaspoon yellow mustard seed

½ teaspoon fenugreek

½ teaspoon turmeric

black pepper

toasted cashew nuts

garam masala

Blend the onion with the garlic and fry in the oil until soft. Add the cumin, coriander, mustard seed, fenugreek and turmeric and stir around for 30 seconds. Add the water, cauliflower and sultanas and season with black pepper. Stir well and bring to the boil, then cover and simmer gently until the cauliflower is just tender. Stir in the ground cashews and continue simmering for a couple of minutes while stirring. Garnish with the toasted cashew nuts and sprinkle with garam masala.

Curried carrot with ginger (*serves 4*)

1½lb/675g carrot, scraped and diced

1 inch/2.5cm piece of root ginger, peeled and chopped

1 onion, peeled and chopped

2 garlic cloves, chopped

1 tablespoon vegetable oil

1 rounded teaspoon cumin seed

1 rounded teaspoon yellow mustard seed

½ teaspoon ground fenugreek

½ teaspoon turmeric

black pepper

6 fl.oz/175ml water

1 inch/2.5cm piece of stem ginger, finely chopped

Blend the root ginger with the onion and garlic, then fry in the oil until golden. Add the cumin and mustard seed, fenugreek and turmeric and stir around for 30 seconds. Put in the carrot and water and season with black pepper. Stir well and bring to the boil, cover and simmer gently for about 25 minutes until cooked. Stir occasionally to prevent sticking. Serve garnished with the chopped stem ginger.

Spiced aubergine with mushrooms in creamy coconut sauce (*serves 4*)

1lb/450g aubergine, diced

8oz/225g button mushrooms, wiped

1 onion, peeled and chopped

2 garlic cloves

2oz/50g creamed coconut, grated

4 tablespoons vegetable oil

6 fl.oz/175ml water

4 fl.oz/125ml soya milk

2 rounded dessertspoons gram flour

2 teaspoons ground coriander

1 teaspoon ground cumin

1 teaspoon turmeric

½ teaspoon fenugreek seed

½ teaspoon paprika

1 inch/2.5cm stick of cinnamon, crushed

black pepper

toasted flaked coconut

Heat the oil in a pan and gently fry the aubergine, onion and garlic for 10 minutes, stirring frequently. Add the coriander, cumin, turmeric, fenugreek seed, paprika, cinnamon and mushrooms and fry for a further minute. Stir in the water, then bring to the boil, cover and simmer gently for 5-10 minutes until the vegetables are tender. Mix the gram flour with the soya milk until smooth and add to the pan together with the creamed coconut. Season with black pepper and bring back to the boil while stirring. Continue stirring for a couple of minutes until the sauce thickens. Use the toasted flaked coconut as garnish when serving.

Dry spiced mixed vegetables *(serves 4)*

1¼lb/550g mixed vegetables (e.g. cauliflower, potato, carrot, parsnip, green beans)

1 red onion, peeled and finely chopped

1 garlic clove, crushed

1 inch/2.5cm piece of root ginger, peeled and finely chopped

2oz/50g tomato, skinned and chopped

1 rounded teaspoon ground coriander

1 rounded teaspoon ground cumin

½ teaspoon turmeric

½ inch/1cm stick of cinnamon, crushed

pinch of ground chilli powder

black pepper

1 tablespoon vegetable oil

4 tablespoons water

finely chopped spring onions

Fry the onion, garlic and ginger in the oil until soft. Add the coriander, cumin, turmeric, cinnamon and chilli powder and stir around for 30 seconds. Chop the vegetables into even-sized small pieces and add them to the pan together with the tomato and water. Season with black pepper and raise the heat. Simmer gently until the vegetables are just done, stirring frequently to prevent sticking. Garnish with spring onions.

Courgettes with peppers *(serves 4)*

12oz/350g courgettes, chopped

3oz/75g red pepper, chopped

3oz/75g green pepper, chopped

6oz/175g tomatoes, skinned and chopped

1 onion, peeled and chopped

2 garlic cloves, crushed

1 small red chilli, finely chopped

1 dessertspoon vegetable oil

1 dessertspoon tamarind purée

1 teaspoon cumin seed

1 teaspoon yellow mustard seed

½ teaspoon turmeric

black pepper

finely chopped fresh coriander leaves

Blend the onion with the garlic and fry with the chilli in the oil until softened. Add the cumin and mustard seed and turmeric and stir around for 30 seconds. Put in the tomatoes and tamarind purée and cook until pulpy, then the courgettes and red and green peppers and season with black pepper. Simmer for about 15 minutes, stirring occasionally, until the vegetables are just tender. Serve garnished with chopped fresh coriander.

Pumpkin, apricot and ginger korma   (serves 4)

1½lb/675g pumpkin flesh, diced

4oz/100g dried apricots, chopped

1oz/25g root ginger, peeled and finely chopped

1 onion, peeled and finely chopped

1 tablespoon vegetable oil

1 rounded dessertspoon korma curry paste

½ teaspoon paprika

¼ teaspoon ground cinnamon

black pepper

8 fl.oz/225ml water

2 rounded tablespoons plain soya yoghurt

toasted flaked almonds

Heat the oil and fry the ginger and onion until soft. Add the curry paste, paprika and cinnamon and stir around for 30 seconds. Now add the pumpkin, apricots and water and season with black pepper. Stir well and bring to the boil. Cover and simmer gently for about 15 minutes until the pumpkin is just cooked. Stir frequently and add a little more water if necessary to prevent sticking. Stir in the yoghurt and continue simmering for a couple of minutes. Garnish with toasted flaked almonds and serve.

Mixed fruit and cashew nut curry   *(serves 4)*

8oz/225g fresh pineapple flesh, diced

2oz/50g dried apricots, finely chopped

2oz/50g dried dates, finely chopped

2oz/50g cashew nuts, ground

2 eating apples, peeled, cored and diced

1 banana, peeled and chopped

1 inch/2.5cm piece of root ginger, peeled and chopped

1 onion, peeled and chopped

1 tablespoon vegetable oil

2 teaspoons garam masala

1 teaspoon mango powder

1 teaspoon fenugreek seed

½ teaspoon coriander seed

8 fl.oz/225ml water

2 tablespoons plain soya yoghurt

toasted cashew nuts

Blend the onion with the ginger, then fry in the oil until soft. Put in the spices and fry for 30 seconds more. Now add the water, pineapple, apricots, dates and apple and stir well. Bring to the boil, cover and simmer for 10 minutes, stirring occasionally, until the apple is just soft. Remove from the heat and stir in the ground cashews, banana and yoghurt. Return to the heat and simmer for a couple of minutes while stirring. Garnish with toasted cashew nuts.

Spinach and mushroom bhajee *(serves 4)*

1lb/450g fresh spinach

4oz/100g button mushrooms, wiped and sliced

1 onion, peeled and finely chopped

1oz/25g vegan margarine

2 teaspoons black mustard seed

1 teaspoon curry powder

1 teaspoon ground coriander

½ teaspoon grated nutmeg

black pepper

6 fl.oz/175ml soya milk

2 rounded tablespoons plain soya yoghurt

Wash the spinach leaves and put them into a large saucepan with only the water that clings to the leaves. Cook gently until tender. Drain and allow to cool, then squeeze out all excess water. Chop the spinach finely and set aside.

Melt the margarine and fry the onion until soft. Add the mustard seed, curry powder, coriander, nutmeg and mushrooms and fry for 2 minutes, then the spinach and soya milk and season with black pepper. Bring to the boil and simmer for 5 minutes, stirring all the time. Remove from the heat and stir in the yoghurt, then gently heat through before serving.

SALADS AND RAITAS

Cool, refreshing salads and raitas are the perfect foil for rich, spicy dishes, which makes them ideal accompaniments for main courses and garnishes for spicy starters. Little bowls of raita or simply plain yoghurt are often served with appetisers, for the spicy foods to be dipped into. Yoghurt is a very important ingredient in Indian cuisine and many families make their own daily for use in sauces, drinks, desserts, bread and savoury snacks.

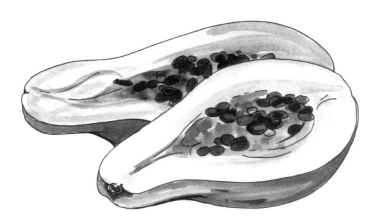

Fruity beansprout and pistachio salad   *(serves 4)*

8oz/225g beansprouts

2oz/50g sultanas

2oz/50g shelled pistachios, chopped

¼oz/7g creamed coconut, grated

1 eating apple, cored and chopped

½ inch/1cm piece of root ginger, peeled and grated

4 cardamoms, husked and the seeds separated

1 dessertspoon vegetable oil

1 dessertspoon lemon juice

chopped fresh coriander leaves

Put the beansprouts in a mixing bowl and add the sultanas, pistachios, coconut, apple, ginger and cardamom seeds. Mix the vegetable oil with the lemon juice and add. Toss very well, then transfer the salad to a serving bowl and garnish with chopped fresh coriander leaves.

Mixed salad   *(serves 4)*

shredded crisp lettuce leaves

3 inch/7.5cm length of cucumber, sliced

2 tomatoes, sliced

1 small carrot, scraped and grated

1 green chilli, finely chopped

2 spring onions, trimmed and finely chopped

dressing

1 tablespoon vegetable oil

1 tablespoon lemon juice

1 dessertspoon light malt vinegar

1 large garlic clove

few sprigs of fresh coriander leaves

black pepper

Spread some shredded lettuce on a round serving plate and arrange the cucumber and tomato slices in a circular pattern on top. Pile the grated carrot in the centre. Put all dressing ingredients in a small blender and blend until smooth. Drizzle the dressing over the salad ingredients and serve garnished with the chopped chilli and spring onions.

Spiced brown lentil salad *(serves 4/6)*

4oz/100g brown lentils

4oz/100g aubergine, finely chopped

4oz/100g red pepper, finely chopped

1oz/25g raisins

1 onion, peeled and finely chopped

2 garlic cloves, crushed

2 tablespoons vegetable oil

1 teaspoon coriander seed, crushed

½ teaspoon cumin seed

¼ teaspoon paprika

½ inch/1cm stick of cinnamon, crushed

4 cardamoms, husked and the seeds separated

black pepper

green salad leaves

chopped fresh coriander leaves

Soak the lentils in water for 2 hours, drain and bring to the boil in a fresh pan of water. Cover and simmer briskly for 20 minutes. Drain again and keep 6 tablespoonfuls of the cooking liquid.

Heat the oil in a large pan and gently fry the aubergine, onion and garlic for 15 minutes. Add the spices, lentils, red pepper, raisins and cooking water. Bring to the boil and simmer uncovered for 5 minutes while stirring. Refrigerate until cold, then serve on a bed of green salad leaves, garnished with chopped fresh coriander.

Onion salad *(serves 4)*

1 red onion, peeled and finely chopped

1 white onion, peeled and finely chopped

1 green chilli, finely chopped

2 tablespoons finely chopped fresh coriander

2 tablespoons lemon juice

1 dessertspoon vegetable oil

black pepper

shredded crisp lettuce leaves

1 tomato, cut into wedges

Mix the onions, chilli and coriander in a large bowl. Combine the lemon juice with the vegetable oil and pour over the salad. Season with black pepper and toss well. Arrange some shredded lettuce leaves on a serving plate and pile the onion salad on top. Garnish with tomato wedges.

Carrot and cumin salad *(serves 4)*

1lb/450g carrots, scraped and grated

1 inch/2.5cm piece of root ginger, peeled and grated

2 teaspoons cumin seed

1 dessertspoon vegetable oil

black pepper

green salad leaves

Dry roast the cumin seed in a heavy-based pan. Add the oil, carrot and ginger and gently fry until just soft. Season with black pepper and put in the fridge until cold. Serve the carrot mixture on a bed of green salad leaves.

Savoury fruit salad (serves 4/6)

8oz/225g tin pineapple cubes in natural juice

1 medium mango, peeled and diced

1 papaya, peeled and diced

1 banana, peeled and sliced

a few black and green seedless grapes, halved

1 inch/2.5cm piece of stem ginger, finely chopped

¼ cucumber, chopped

lemon juice

1 rounded teaspoon tamarind purée

½ teaspoon chilli powder

black pepper

fresh mint leaves

Sprinkle the banana with lemon juice and put in a mixing bowl with the mango, papaya, grapes, ginger and cucumber. Drain the pineapple cubes and keep 2 tablespoonfuls of juice. Add the cubes to the bowl. Mix the tamarind purée with the pineapple juice and pour over the salad. Add the chilli powder and season with black pepper. Toss well, then spoon into a serving bowl and garnish with fresh mint leaves.

Potato korma salad (serves 4)

1½ lb/675g new potatoes, scraped

6 spring onions, trimmed and sliced

4 rounded tablespoons plain soya yoghurt

1 rounded dessertspoon korma curry paste

black pepper

chopped fresh coriander leaves

Boil the potatoes until done, drain and rinse under cold running water. Drain well, dice and put in a large bowl. Mix the curry paste with the yoghurt until smooth and spoon the dressing over the potatoes. Add the spring onions and season with black pepper. Combine thoroughly and transfer the salad to a serving dish. Cover and chill for a couple of hours. Serve garnished with chopped coriander.

Curried mushroom salad (serves 4)

12oz/350g button mushrooms, wiped and halved

2 garlic cloves, crushed

4 rounded tablespoons plain soya yoghurt

1 rounded dessertspoon curry paste

1 dessertspoon vegetable oil

black pepper

shredded crisp lettuce leaves

1 green chilli, finely chopped

Heat the oil and gently fry the garlic. Add the mushrooms and fry for another minute, then transfer to a mixing bowl. Combine the curry paste with the yoghurt and spoon over the mushrooms. Season with black pepper and mix until the mushrooms are coated in the dressing. Chill for a couple of hours, then arrange the salad on a bed of shredded lettuce and garnish with the chopped chilli.

Garlic and herb raita (serves 4)

6 fl.oz/175ml plain soya yoghurt

2 garlic cloves, crushed

1 tablespoon finely chopped fresh mint

1 tablespoon finely chopped fresh coriander

black pepper

2 spring onions, trimmed and finely chopped

Mix the yoghurt with the garlic, mint and coriander. Season with black pepper and spoon into a serving bowl. Garnish with spring onions.

Banana raita   *(serves 4)*

1 just ripe banana, peeled

6 fl.oz/175ml plain soya yoghurt

1 dessertspoon demerara sugar

lemon juice

garam masala

Cut the banana in half. Mash one half and chop the other. Sprinkle the banana with lemon juice and add to the yoghurt together with the demerara sugar. Put in a serving bowl and sprinkle with garam masala.

Cucumber and coriander raita   *(serves 4)*

6 fl.oz/175ml plain soya yoghurt

4oz/100g cucumber, finely chopped

2 rounded tablespoons chopped fresh coriander leaves

black pepper

few red chilli rings

Mix the cucumber and coriander with the yoghurt, season with black pepper and transfer to a serving bowl. Garnish with a few red chilli rings.

Fruity raita   (serves 4)

1 banana, peeled and chopped

2oz/50g seedless grapes, halved

4 no-soak dried apricots, chopped

1oz/25g sultanas

1 tablespoon fresh orange juice

1 dessertspoon demerara sugar

6 fl.oz/175ml plain soya yoghurt

½ teaspoon garam masala

Soak the sultanas in the orange juice for 30 minutes, then mix well with the other ingredients and spoon into a serving bowl.

Vegetable raita   (serves 4)

6 fl.oz/175ml plain soya yoghurt

2oz/50g green pepper, finely chopped

2oz/50g red pepper, finely chopped

1 small onion, peeled and grated

1 garlic clove, crushed

1 tomato, skinned and chopped

1 tablespoon vegetable oil

1 teaspoon ground coriander

black pepper

chopped fresh coriander leaves

Heat the oil and gently fry the green and red pepper, onion and garlic until softened. Add the ground coriander and stir around for 30 seconds. Refrigerate until cold, then add the tomato and season with black pepper. Mix in the yoghurt until well combined. Transfer to a serving dish and garnish with chopped fresh coriander.

CHUTNEYS

Chutneys have always been a popular accompaniment for curries, especially with the British, who brought recipes back with them when they returned to Britain. Used to add both contrasting and complementing flavours and colour to the meal, chutneys are also served with spicy starters and snack foods. Both fruit- and vegetable-based chutneys are easy to make and they are a good way of preserving produce when there is a glut. Chutneys are best stored for a couple of weeks before use to allow the flavours to mature.

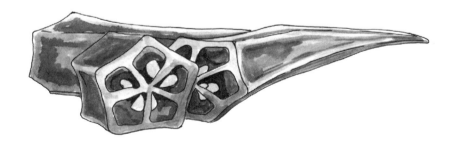

Mango and ginger chutney
(makes approx. 3 lb/1.5kg)

2lb/900g mangoes, peeled and chopped

4oz/100g stem ginger, finely chopped

1 onion, peeled and grated

6 fl.oz/175ml light malt vinegar

4oz/100g demerara sugar

1 teaspoon yellow mustard seed

¼ teaspoon ground cardamom

Put the ingredients in a large saucepan and stir well. Bring to the boil, then simmer gently uncovered for 35-40 minutes until the mixture reduces down and thickens. Stir frequently to prevent sticking. Spoon the chutney into warm sterilised jars and cover.

Aubergine, apple and date chutney
(makes approx. 2½ lb/1.1kg)

12oz/350g aubergine, finely chopped

12oz/350g cooking apple, peeled, cored and finely chopped

4oz/100g dried dates, finely chopped

1 onion, peeled and finely chopped

14 fl.oz/400ml light malt vinegar

4oz/100g demerara sugar

1 dessertspoon tamarind purée

1 teaspoon black mustard seed

½ teaspoon ground coriander

¼ teaspoon ground fenugreek

¼ teaspoon ground cinnamon

Put the aubergine, onion and 10 fl.oz/300ml of vinegar in a large saucepan. Bring to the boil, cover and simmer for 10 minutes. Remove from the heat and add the remaining ingredients. Stir well, then return to the heat and bring back to the boil. Simmer gently for about 30 minutes until the mixture reduces and thickens, stirring frequently to prevent sticking. Spoon into warm sterilised jars and cover.

Peach and sultana chutney *(makes approx. 3lb/1.5kg)*

2½lb/1.1kg firm peaches, stoned and finely chopped

8oz/225g sultanas

8oz/225g onion, peeled and finely chopped

6oz/175g demerara sugar

10 fl.oz/300ml light malt vinegar

1 rounded teaspoon garam masala

Put the ingredients in a large saucepan and stir well. Bring to the boil, then simmer gently for about 45 minutes uncovered, stirring frequently, until the mixture reduces down and thickens. Spoon the chutney into warm sterilised jars and cover.

Spiced apple chutney *(makes approx. 3lb/1.5kg)*

2½lb/1.1kg cooking apples, peeled, cored and chopped

8oz/225g onion, peeled and finely chopped

8oz/225g demerara sugar

4oz/100g sultanas

1oz/25g root ginger, peeled and finely chopped

10 fl.oz/300ml light malt vinegar

1 dessertspoon yellow mustard seed

1 rounded teaspoon ground coriander

1 rounded teaspoon ground cumin

1 teaspoon turmeric

¼ teaspoon chilli powder

¼ teaspoon ground cardamom

Put all the ingredients in a large saucepan, stir well and bring to the boil. Simmer uncovered for about 45 minutes until the mixture reduces and thickens. Stir frequently to prevent sticking. Spoon into warm sterilised jars and cover.

Apricot and banana chutney
(makes approx. 3lb/1.5kg)

2½lb/1.1kg fresh apricots, stoned and chopped

2 firm bananas, peeled and chopped

2oz/50g stem ginger, finely chopped

1 onion, peeled and finely chopped

4oz/100g demerara sugar

8 fl.oz/225ml light malt vinegar

¼ teaspoon ground mace

¼ teaspoon ground cinnamon

Combine all the ingredients in a large saucepan. Bring to the boil and while stirring frequently simmer gently uncovered for about 45 minutes. Once the mixture has reduced and thickened, spoon it into warm sterilised jars and cover.

DESSERTS

Although many restaurants offer the following types of dessert to round off a meal, a typical Indian family might have just a piece of fruit or a fruit salad, preferring to eat sweet dishes at other times of the day as a snack. Many Indian sweet dishes are milk- and yoghurt-based and vegan substitutes work admirably to produce an authentic taste. The stuffed pastries are a speciality from Gujarat and are like samosas but with a sweet filling. One of the most popular sweet dishes is kheer, a spiced rice pudding with almonds. Chopped fruit is sometimes added when it is served cold.

Tropical fruit salad   *(serves 4)*

    14oz/400g tin guavas in syrup
    1 papaya, peeled and diced
    1 medium mango, peeled and diced
    1 banana, peeled and sliced
    1 passion fruit
    a few black seedless grapes, halved
    lemon juice
    2 inch/5cm cinnamon stick
    6 cloves
    toasted flaked coconut

Chop the guavas and put them in a mixing bowl with the syrup, papaya, mango and grapes. Sprinkle the banana with lemon juice and add together with the cinnamon stick and cloves. Scoop out the flesh and seeds from the passion fruit and add to the salad. Mix well, cover and chill for a couple of hours. Remove the cinnamon stick and cloves and serve the salad garnished with toasted flaked coconut.

Banana shrikand   *(serves 4)*

    8oz/225g vegan 'cream cheese'
    8 fl.oz/225ml plain soya yoghurt
    2oz/50g icing sugar
    1 large ripe banana, peeled and chopped
    pinch of ground saffron
    ½ teaspoon ground cardamom
    toasted flaked almonds

Put the 'cream cheese', yoghurt, icing sugar, saffron and cardamom in a mixing bowl and beat until well combined. Stir in the banana and divide the mixture between 4 serving bowls. Garnish with toasted flaked almonds.

Guava and mango sharbat *(serves 4)*

14oz/400g tin of guavas in syrup

14oz/400g tin of mango in syrup

5oz/150ml plain soya yoghurt

Drain the tinned fruit over a bowl. Mix the juices and pour into a freezerproof container, then freeze for a few hours until solid. Chop the guavas and mango, mix and chill until ready to serve.

Put the frozen juice into a plastic food bag and place between a clean tea towel on a chopping board. Hit the ice with a rolling pin until it is crushed. Divide the crushed ice between 4 serving glasses, add the fruit and spoon the yoghurt on top.

Almond kulfi *(serves 4)*

9 fl.oz/250ml soya 'cream'

3 fl.oz/75ml plain soya yoghurt

4oz/100g ground almonds

1 rounded tablespoon caster sugar

½ teaspoon almond essence

tropical fruits

toasted flaked almonds

Put the soya 'cream' and yoghurt in a blender with the ground almonds, sugar and almond essence. Blend briefly until smooth, then transfer to a shallow freezerproof container. Cover and freeze for a few hours. Keep at room temperature for 30 minutes before serving if the kulfi has frozen too solidly. Serve with tropical fruits and garnish with toasted flaked almonds.

Kheer *(serves 4)*

2oz/50g ground rice

1oz/25g demerara sugar

½ oz/15g sultanas

½ oz/15g flaked almonds, toasted and chopped

¼ teaspoon ground cinnamon

pinch of ground cardamom

1 rounded dessertspoon vegan margarine

20 fl.oz/600ml soya milk

Melt the margarine in a heavy-based pan. Add the cinnamon, cardamom and rice and stir around for 1 minute. Pour in three-quarters of the soya milk and combine thoroughly. Bring to the boil while stirring, then remove from the heat and stir in the sugar, remaining soya milk, sultanas and three-quarters of the chopped almonds. Bring back to the boil whilst stirring and continue stirring for 3-4 minutes until the mixture thickens. Divide the kheer between 4 dishes and serve hot or cold, garnished with the remaining almonds.

Apricot and coconut yoghurt puddings *(serves 4)*

8oz/225g no-soak dried apricots

16 fl.oz/475ml water

10 fl.oz/300ml plain soya yoghurt

1oz/25g creamed coconut, grated

1 tablespoon demerara sugar

toasted flaked coconut

Put the apricots and water in a saucepan and bring to the boil. Cover and simmer gently for about 20 minutes until soft. Allow to cool, then pour the apricots and cooking liquid into a blender. Add the yoghurt, creamed coconut and sugar and blend until smooth. Spoon into 4 glasses, cover and chill. Garnish each dessert with toasted flaked coconut when serving

---

Mango and lime sorbet   *(serves 4)*

> 1 medium just ripe mango, peeled and chopped
> 8 fl.oz/225ml water
> 1oz/25g demerara sugar
> 2 tablespoons lime juice

Put all the ingredients in a saucepan and bring to the boil. Simmer for about 5 minutes until the mango is soft. Allow to cool slightly, then liquidise until smooth. Pour into a shallow freezerproof tray and cover. Freeze for 2 hours, then whisk and put back in the freezer until frozen. Keep at room temperature for 30 minutes before serving if the sorbet has become too hard.

Carrot and almond pudding   *(serves 4)*

> 1¼lb/550g carrots, scraped and grated
> 16 fl.oz/475ml soya milk
> 2oz/50g flaked almonds, toasted
> 1oz/25g sultanas
> 1oz/25g raisins
> 1oz/25g demerara sugar
> pinch of ground cardamom

Keep a few flaked almonds for garnishing and finely chop the rest. Put the carrots and soya milk in a saucepan and bring to the boil. Cover and simmer gently for about 45 minutes, stirring occasionally, until the milk has been absorbed . Add the chopped almonds and remaining ingredients and cook for a further 3 minutes while stirring. Spoon into glasses and serve either hot or cold, sprinkled with the remaining flaked almonds.

Banana and coconut nimki (serves 4/6)

6oz/175g plain wholewheat flour

1 ripe banana (approx. 6oz/175g), peeled and mashed

1oz/25g creamed coconut, grated

½ oz/15g vegan margarine

¼ teaspoon ground cinnamon

water

vegetable oil

hot sugar syrup (optional)

Mix the cinnamon with the flour and rub in the margarine. Add the coconut and banana and combine thoroughly. Add a little cold water and mix until a soft dough forms. Knead well and turn out onto a floured board. Roll out thinly and cut into little diagonal shapes. Prick the tops with a fork and fry in hot oil until golden. Drain on kitchen paper and dip in hot sugar syrup if wished. Serve hot.

Sweet stuffed pastries (makes 8)

pastry

5oz/150g self-raising flour

2oz/50g vegan margarine

½ teaspoon ground cinnamon

water

vegetable oil

filling

2oz/50g charoli or mixed nuts, finely chopped

2oz/50g ground rice

1oz/25g sultanas

1oz/25g creamed coconut, grated

½ oz/15g demerara sugar

1 rounded dessertspoon vegan margarine

4 tablespoons soya milk

¼ teaspoon ground cardamom

Make the pastry by mixing the cinnamon with the flour and rubbing in the margarine. Add enough cold water to make a soft dough. Knead well, divide the dough into 8 equal pieces and roll each one out into a 3½inch/9cm circle.

Mix the nuts with the ground rice, sultanas, coconut, sugar and cardamom. Melt the margarine in a saucepan, remove from the heat and stir in the nut mixture. Add the soya milk and stir until everything binds together. Divide the mixture between the pastry circles, placing it neatly on one side only. Dampen the edges of the pastry with water and fold in half to enclose the filling. Press the edges together to join and neaten them. Fry the pastries in hot vegetable oil for a few minutes on each side until golden brown. Drain on kitchen paper and serve hot.

DRINKS

Long, cool, refreshing drinks offer a welcome respite in India's hot climate and together with snack foods they are readily available from roadside stalls. Sherbets and lassis are often served with appetisers at the start of a meal, while masala, a spiced tea, is traditionally served at the end of a meal. Coffee topped with ice cream is a south Indian speciality and is served in coffee houses throughout the region.

Pineapple sherbet (serves 4)

8oz/225g peeled fresh pineapple, chopped

20 fl.oz/600ml water

1 rounded tablespoon demerara sugar

fresh pineapple cubes

Put the pineapple, water and sugar in a blender and blend until smooth. Pour through a strainer into a jug. Cover and keep in the fridge for a few hours. Stir well, pour into glasses and add a few pineapple cubes to each glass.

Sparkling peach sherbet (serves 4)

14oz/400g tin peaches in syrup

20 fl.oz/600ml sparkling mineral water

crushed ice

Blend the peaches and syrup until smooth. Pour into a large jug and stir in the mineral water. Serve in tumblers with crushed ice.

Lemon sherbet (serves 4)

juice of 2 lemons

24 fl.oz/725ml water

1 rounded tablespoon caster sugar

crushed ice

mint leaves

Mix the lemon juice and caster sugar with the water until the sugar dissolves. Pour into glasses and add crushed ice. Garnish with mint leaves.

Green grape sherbet (serves 4)

8oz/225g large green seedless grapes, skinned and chopped

22 fl.oz/650ml water

1 rounded dessertspoon caster sugar

ice cubes

green grapes

Blend the grapes with the water and caster sugar until smooth. Pass through a fine sieve into a jug, pressing through any remaining purée with the back of a spoon. Stir well, then pour into glasses and add ice cubes. Garnish each glass with green grapes.

Melon and lime lassi (serves 4)

8oz/225g melon flesh, chopped

2 dessertspoons lime juice

8 fl.oz/225ml plain soya yoghurt

2 dessertspoons caster sugar

4 fl.oz/125ml soya milk

4 fl.oz/125ml water

crushed ice

lime slices

Blend the melon with the lime juice, yoghurt, sugar, soya milk and water until smooth. Pour into glasses garnished with a slice of lime and add crushed ice.

Banana and coconut lassi   *(serves 4)*

1 large ripe banana, peeled and chopped

16 fl.oz/475ml water

4 fl.oz/125ml plain soya yoghurt

½ oz/15g creamed coconut, grated

½ oz/15g caster sugar

crushed ice

ground cinnamon

Put the banana, water, yoghurt, coconut and sugar in a blender and blend until smooth. Pass through a fine sieve into a jug. Pour into glasses, add crushed ice and sprinkle the top of each drink lightly with ground cinnamon.

Mango and orange lassi   *(serves 4)*

6oz/175g ripe mango flesh

6 fl.oz/175ml plain soya yoghurt

9 fl.oz/250ml water

10 fl.oz/300ml fresh orange juice

½ oz/15g caster sugar

crushed ice

orange slices

Blend the mango flesh, yoghurt, water, orange juice and sugar until smooth. Pour into glasses and add crushed ice. Garnish each glass with a slice of orange.

Almond and saffron milk   *(serves 4)*

28 fl.oz/825ml sweetened soya milk

1oz/25g ground almonds

¼ teaspoon ground saffron

¼ teaspoon ground cardamom

crushed ice

Blend the soya milk with the almonds, saffron and cardamom. Pour into a jug and whisk slightly until frothy. Serve in tumblers and add crushed ice.

Iced masala tea   *(serves 4)*

24 fl.oz/725ml boiling strong black tea

12 cloves

8 cardamom pods, husked and the seeds separated

2 inch/5cm stick of cinnamon

demerara sugar (optional)

ice cubes

Crush the spices lightly with a pestle in a mortar. Add to the boiling tea and stir, adding a little sugar to sweeten if desired. Cover and refrigerate until cold. Strain the tea into glasses and add ice cubes.

Iced coffee cream

(serves 4)

30 fl.oz/900ml black coffee

demerara sugar (optional)

4 scoops of vegan vanilla ice cream

ground cinnamon

Sweeten the coffee with sugar if wished, cover and keep in the fridge until cold. Pour the coffee into 4 glasses, add a scoop of vanilla ice cream to each one and sprinkle with ground cinnamon.

More Vegan Cookbooks by Linda Majzlik

Vegan Dinner Parties

"If no one has yet told you that vegan food is varied, healthy and scrumptious, this is just the book for you. The author's choice of genuinely cruelty-free ingredients varies from the more exotic to the re-assuringly homely, but they all stimulate the taste buds and they're all available on the high street."

Vegan food is much in demand as more people are advised to avoid dairy products for health reasons. It is also a logical next choice after becoming a vegetarian, since meat is not the only animal product dependent on cruelty and abuse. So these recipes avoid the use of milk, butter, cream, honey and eggs, as well as meat and its by-products.

All the recipes are tried and tested. Although they are organised into monthly menus, you can of course pick and choose to make up menus and dishes for any occasion.

£5.99 paperback   96pp   1 897766 46 7

Illustrated with cartoons by Mark Blanford

"For the sake of the world, its people and its animals, it is important to reclaim our food from those who pretend that pain and suffering are an essential part of our diet. Enjoy these great recipes because they strike a blow for the oppressed of the world — humans and animals alike."

From the Foreword by Juliet Gellatley, founder and director of Viva!

Vegan Barbecues and Buffets

Having a barbecue on a hot summer's day? Laying on a buffet for a crowded event? The vegan choice is simply great!

From mushroom and pine kernel sausages and smoked tofu and mushroom medallions, a sunflower and soya loaf and aubergine and brazil nut paté to a tempting assortment of salads, spreads and dips, and an array of sumptuous desserts, Linda Majzlik takes you on a festive journey of vegan delights that will appeal to every palate, yet remains completely wholesome and cruelty-free from beginning to end.

A lot of the preparation can be done in advance: many of the recipes are suitable for freezing, while others can be kept in the fridge. So the cook can enjoy the day as much as the guests!

£5.99 paperback   96pp   1 897766 55 6

Vegan Baking

Includes over 100 recipes for cakes, loaves, biscuits, tray bakes, no-bake cakes and savoury baking – all free of animal products and all tried and tested.

£5.99 paperback   96pp   1 897766 63 7

'The book that every vegan has been waiting for …
the kind of cookery book that you wouldn't get bored with …
a very useful addition to any kitchen.' *The Vegan*

'Very good.' *The Vegetarian*

A Vegan Taste of the Caribbean

Appetisers, soups and stews, accompaniments for soups, stews and curries, main courses, rice, vegetables, salads, chutneys, salsas and sauces, desserts, baking, drinks. Over 100 recipes, plus what to keep in the Caribbean storecupboard.

'A taste of magic.' *The Vegetarian*

£5.99 paperback   112 pp   1 897766 70 X

What they wrote about *Vegan Dinner Parties*:

'Imaginative... very good value' *The Vegan*

'Linda's tasty book runs through the twelve months of the year with a mouth-watering and well-balanced three-course meal for each one' *Wildlife Guardian*

'This inspiring book proves just how sophisticated and tasty vegan food can be' *Agscene*

'Superb idea – a book long overdue' *Green World*

A Vegan Taste of Italy

Starters, soups, sauces, risottos, main courses (inlcuding stuffed vegetables, pizza, pasta, and vegeatbles), salads and desserts, and baking (Focaccia, breadsticks, panforte, macaroons, etc.). Over 120 recipes, all free of animal products.

'Over 120 recipes to delight and enthrall you.' *The Vegetarian*

£5.99 paperback   128 pp   1 897766 65 3

A Vegan Taste of Mexico

Soups, dips and snacks, authentic sauces, salsas and rice dishes, recipes for main courses and vegetable side dishes, together with salads, desserts, cakes and cookies — these 130 recipes remain true to the tasty culinary traditions of Mexico, but avoid animal ingredients.

£5.99   paperback   1 897766 71 8

Information on how to order can be found on the back of the title page of this book.